Praise for Chasing Simple Marketing

"A permission slip to stress less and focus more on what matters - Amanda provides a clear roadmap on how you can grow your business without spending all of your time and energy on marketing." - *Natalie Franke, Author of Built to Belong and Gutsy*

"In a world where business feels more and more complicated each day, Amanda keeps marketing simple. Chasing Simple Marketing strips away the comparison traps and 'shoulds' of business marketing. Instead, she delivers an honest, insightful look into how to market your business without burning yourself out. If you're looking for a sustainable way to market your business for the long haul - look no further." - *Jessica Rasdall, Author of Shattered, Public Speaking Coach, and Host of the Speak to Scale Podcast*

"If you love to work harder, not smarter - don't read this book! Amanda does a fabulous job of distilling sometimes intimidating marketing strategies and confusing jargon into a super simple, easy-to-read guidebook. Plus, her top-notch storytelling makes it feel like a conversation with a friend over coffee. If you own a business and want it to grow without wasting tons of time in the process, you NEED this book!" - *Anna Dearmon Kornick, Time Management Coach, Host of It's About Time Podcast, and Author of Time Management Essentials*

"Chasing Simple Marketing will teach you a lot more than how to spend less time on your content marketing. Amanda breaks down overwhelming concepts and explains them in simple-to-grasp ways - there's no fluff or sugar-coating here! You no longer have to struggle with a lack of business growth with this practical guide. If you're looking for a foundational guide for simplifying your marketing strategy, this is it!" - *Laylee Emadi Smith, Founder of the Creative Educator Conference*

Chasing Simple Marketing

A Crash Course in Content Marketing for Showing Up, Saving Time, and Growing Your Business

Amanda Warfield

AIKEN, SC

DOWNLOAD YOUR AUDIO BOOK FREE!

As a thank you for purchasing my book, I'd love to gift you the Audiobook version - 100% free!

I know you're a busy entrepreneur, and sitting down to read might be difficult. My hope is that by gifting you this version, you'll be able to listen on the go and easily read the book. That way, you can start implementing what's inside, and simplify your marketing a whole lot faster!

AMANDAWARFIELD.COM/AUDIO

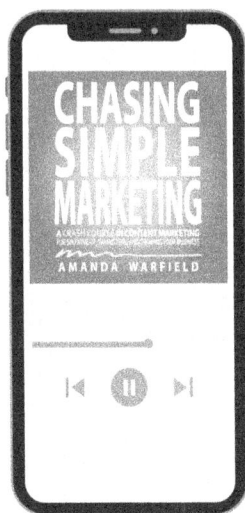

WANT MORE MARKETING CONTENT?

Tune in to Chasing Simple, the podcast to make marketing simple and less time consuming. So that you can spend less time marketing and more time growing your business, and doing what you love.

Meet me in your favorite podcast player each week for love, support, practical tips and advice on uncomplicating your marketing and business. Let's do this entrepreneurship thing together, shall we?

AMANDAWARFIELD.COM/CHASING-SIMPLE

SIMPLIFY YOUR CONTENT MARKETING

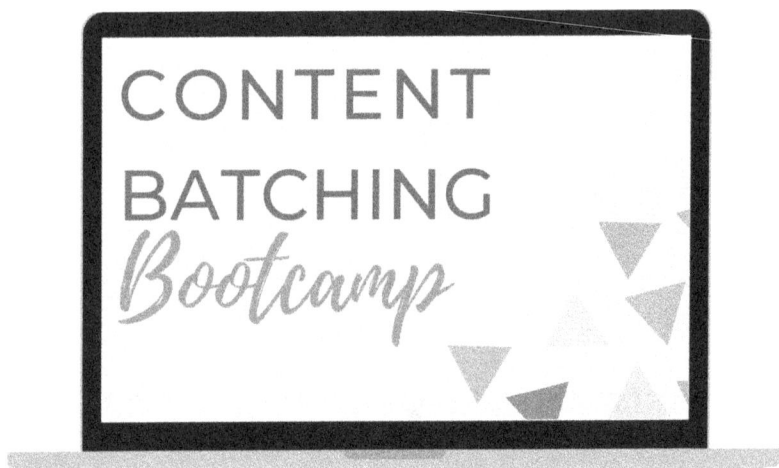

CONTENT
BATCHING
Bootcamp

WANT MY HELP IMPLEMENTING THE CONTENT IN THIS BOOK?

Content Batching Bootcamp is an online course that helps entrepreneurs create a content batching system that's unique to their own business, get off the content creation hamster wheel by becoming consistent with their content in order to build relationships with their audience and grow their bottom line so that they can build the business that will support their dream life.

Students inside of Content Batching Bootcamp learn how to create a batching system that works for their unique business (whether they work five hours a week or forty), and they have seen remarkable results from only having to create content once a month.

If you want to get off the content creation hamster wheel, and see results from what you read in this book even faster, Content Batching Bootcamp will get you there even quicker:

AMANDAWARFIELD.COM/CONTENT

Published by Girardeau Publishing, a division of Amanda Warfield, LLC.

Girardeau Publishing

PO Box 6822 Aiken, SC 29804

girardeaupublishing.com

First Edition: July 2023

For more information, email hello@amandawarfield.com

Library of Congress Control Number: 2023912150

ISBNs: 979-8-9884886-0-6 (hardcover) | 979-8-9884886-1-3 (paperback) | 979-8-9884886-2-0 (ebook)

To Russell, for loving me for me, for always making me laugh when I'm neck-deep in overwhelm, and for not hesitating to support my wild dream six years ago - and every day since.

My love you forever.

Table of Contents

Introduction 1

Section 1 : Master Content Marketing Foundations

    Chapter One: Crash Course in Marketing 11

    Chapter Two: Your Marketing Permission Slip 33

    Chapter Three: Build It and They Won't Come 43

    Chapter Four: Marketing Practices to Discard 63

    Chapter Five: Leverage Growth Strategies 75

    Chapter Six: Educate. Entertain. Connect. Sell. 95

Section 2: Clarify Your Business Journey

    Chapter Seven: Content Creator Phase 107

    Chapter Eight: Foundation Builder Phase 121

    Chapter Nine: Established Entrepreneur Phase 133

Section 3: Simplify For Consistency

    Chapter Ten: Content is Not Your Business 151

    Chapter Eleven: Create Less Content 167

    Chapter Twelve: Become a Broken Record 179

    Chapter Thirteen: Batch Your Content 215

Conclusion: What's Next? 235

Acknowledgements 245

Appendix 249

Notes 251

INTRODUCTION

I started batching my content because a dog had peed on our carpets.

My husband and I had just moved into our new home, and as we were moving in our furniture and unpacking boxes, we learned that things were not as they seemed during all of our pre-closing walk-throughs. We had been so excited about the condition of the carpets, but as we went from room to room, it became apparent that the previous owner's dog had peed on every.single.carpet. in the house.

Now is probably a good time to mention that we're cat people. Meaning that as we were unloading all of our things - the very first two "things" to be unpacked were our cats.

And cats? Well, they can be a bit territorial. We were very nervous that one or both cats would sniff those dried-up pee spots and decide to mark their territory right over the top. Which could lead to bad litter box habits for a lifetime that I had absolutely zero interest in struggling with.

After renting a carpet cleaner and deep cleaning each carpet without any luck, we decided the only reasonable next step would be to rip out all of the carpets and start over. Because we didn't want to have any issues with the cats, we ripped the carpets out within days of moving in.

But we had another problem. Due to some renovations happening in our bedroom, we couldn't put the new carpet back in (since we wanted to do it all at once). For six months, we had three rooms in our house with just a subfloor.

Including? My office.

If you're a podcaster, you may already know where I'm going with this. But, if not, sound quality is crucial for those of us with audio-based content. So much so that it's not uncommon for podcasters to record inside their closets because all of the clothes hanging there are great at muffling extra sounds. And subflooring? It's the opposite of helpful for sound quality.

So, I gathered up every blanket we owned and spread them across the top of my desk and all over the floor to soften the echoes and extra sounds. It wasn't perfect (which you'd hear if you listen to the early episodes of my podcast - Chasing Simple), but it was a night and day difference from only the subfloor.

When it was time to record my upcoming episode each week, I'd pull out all the blankets, spread them around, and get to work. Then, I'd pick them all back up again and put them away.

As I'm sure you can imagine, this got old *quickly*. I tried leaving the blankets out, but they shifted around (and got dirty) from being walked all over. So I scrapped that idea, too.

Since we were a few months in, I was sure that the master renovation would be wrapping up any time now and that by the next month, we would have carpet. I was convinced that I wouldn't have this problem much longer.

So, I thought, *why don't I record enough episodes for the next month all at once?* Then, I'll have carpet and be able to get back to recording one at a time so that I'm not spending all day recording.

And, boy, did it feel good only to have to pull those blankets out once in the entire month. (Not to mention, there was so much relief over the next three weeks in not having to deal with recording a new episode).

And then the next month came, and renovations still weren't done. So I thought, okay - *this* will be the final month. I'll record a month's worth of episodes in a day one more time.

And the same thing happened again the next month, and the next.

At which point, I'd gotten adventurous. You see, my brain LOVES to organize and systematize things. After a couple of months of batch recording episodes - I loved that I could set aside a day just for recording and not worry about it every week. So I wondered if I could do that with the rest of my content.

And over the next few months, I did just that. I tweaked my systems and processes until I could create a month's worth of content in one week. This left me free to work **on** my business, not just **in** it for the other three weeks of each month.

Coincidentally, I started to see mega-growth in my business around the same time I started batching.

I found that my messaging was more consistent when I created it all at once.

I found that showing up consistently led to higher engagement rates.

I found that when I didn't need to think about marketing, I had so much more space to make progress elsewhere in my business.

Content batching was my gateway to an infatuation with content marketing. One that led to years of discovery and growth, a wide variety of clients, and a vastly different bottom line.

And think. I started batching my content because a dog had peed on our carpets.

Who This Book Is For

And now, dear friend - may I call you friend? I feel like if you've read this far, you practically fought the pee battle alongside us, which automatically makes you a friend in my book - I'm here to share all that I've learned with *you* so that you can take your content from non-existent or inconsistent, to a true tool to grow your business.

Because I wrote this book for the newer business owner. The one that has stumbled into entrepreneurship because they were following their passion. But without a Masters of Business Administration (MBA) or background in business, they find marketing overwhelming and frustrating.

Since you picked up this book, I'm guessing that your content marketing goes a little something like this:

You try to devise some sort of plan each month for what you will talk about. You've tried buckets, you've tried themes, and you feel like you've tried it all.

You can sing every word of the *Moana* soundtrack. And yet, knowing what to say to your audience? It's a dusty, empty attic up there in your brain.

Once you finally put something together for your plan, you've got to create the content itself. You've set aside one day each week to create your content, and sometimes it works. You sit down and get everything created for the entire week and scheduled to go out.

But most of the time? Something comes up. Your kid gets sick, or you get sick. A client needs you. You're behind on other tasks. An important project holds a higher priority. So, you put the content off until the last minute. And you end every day either scrambling to create and post something or shrugging your shoulders and telling yourself tomorrow; you'll finally post again for the first time in months.

Content marketing doesn't feel all that important - until you realize that your client roster is starting to get a little thin and the leads aren't coming in like they used to. So, you get serious about creating content again. Just until you fill your roster back up, that is.

But in your gut. You KNOW that your marketing is essential, and you want to get a handle on yours. You want to see growth and client leads, and you want the entire process to be simple.

What to Expect

As we take this journey together, there are two things you can expect from this book: 1) vulnerability and 2) simplicity.

If you listen to my podcast, Chasing Simple, you'll already know I'm passionate about sharing the hard parts of entrepreneurship. Because as much as we would all like to believe that we can hit six figures overnight, most of us have found that's not the case. Building a solid business takes time, and it takes work. And within that time and hard work, there are hard days.

One of the first things I noticed about marketing is how over-whelming and complicated it's made out to be. Whether working on my own marketing, client's marketing, or helping my students, I always ask myself, "How can I make it as simple as possible while also seeing growth?"

I promise that you will get the vulnerable truth as you read this book and hear my stories.

I promise you will walk away feeling confident about your content marketing.

And I promise you'll walk away with an actionable plan for simpli-fying *so that you can fit your marketing into your business without it taking over your business.*

Throughout these pages, I will take you on a simplicity-focused journey to improve your content marketing. We'll start in Section One with a crash course in content marketing so that we're on the same page and you have a solid foundation to build your marketing. In all likelihood, you may be GREAT at marketing, but you're over-whelmed because you don't have the foundations in place to know that you are.

In Section Two, we'll go over exactly where you should focus your marketing and which strategies will work best for your business based on your business phase.

As we head into Section Three, we'll dive deep into consistency. Because without consistency, none of the other things matter. I'll share my three steps for simplifying your content marketing in order to be able to show up consistently.

And finally, we'll end our journey together with the next steps you can take. I'll show you how you can implement these strategies and share a few extra tips for getting your marketing done even quicker.

I hope that by laying the groundwork out for you, you can take what you learn in this book and run with it.

You'll be able to simplify your marketing so that you can get consistent without sacrificing your needle-moving or client-serving time.

Marketing will stop being something to fear and instead become something fun.

And you'll be able to fit your marketing into your business without it taking over your business.

I've helped over 150 business owners do exactly that, and now it's your turn. Let's get started uncomplicating your marketing, shall we?

At the end of each chapter, I will share two things with you:

1) Action Steps based on what you learned in that chapter.

2) Additional Resources you can utilize to take what you've learned in that chapter to the next level.

Action Step:

Take a minute and journal what you hope to accomplish once you've learned how to leverage your marketing best.

Additional Resources:

For full resources in one place, head to:
https://amandawarfield.com/chasing-simple-marketing-bonuses/

SECTION 1

MASTER CONTENT MARKETING FOUNDATIONS

ONE
CRASH COURSE IN MARKETING

For about a week, I'd gone back and forth, talking myself in and out of doing my idea. It was time to talk to my husband about it.

Deep breath.

"I want to start a blog."

Another deep breath.

"A blog that I'm going to turn into a business."

One more deep breath.

"And it's going to cost us about a thousand dollars to get started."

Quick! Blurt it out!

"But hopefully I'm going to make money with it someday."

My husband's response?

"Okay."

Had he been paying attention to me? I mean, who do I think I am, right? Why would anyone listen to what *I* have to say on a blog? What would I even talk about on a blog? And make money from it? How? Who would pay me?

"Okay? That's it? Just okay??"

I kid you not. This man looked me in the eyes and said, "I believe in you, baby. If this is what you want, I support you."

Flashback to about a week earlier - I'd felt a nudge to start a blog on simplicity. And when I pushed that nudge away, I'd gotten a couple more nudges throughout the week at various points—which I kept pushing away until finally, I realized that I couldn't ignore the idea any longer.

Mind you, this was long after the blogging heyday - when you could type up a post and grow a following based on your lifestyle. By this point, blogs were being used for search engine optimization (SEO) purposes and no longer for connection.

All I had was my nudge and some vague idea about how I was going to turn a blog into a business.

For the next year, I spent all my spare hours before and after work trying to build a business out of our guest room. I'd wake up, spend an hour or so checking things off my to-do list, head into my "real" job as a preschool teacher, and then once I was off the clock, I'd rush home (absorbing as many business podcast episodes on the way as possible) to put in more hours.

Truthfully, it sounds a lot more glamorous in writing than it was at the time. Those first few months were spent doing two main tasks - researching and marketing. Since I knew nothing about marketing or creating a business, I spent hours and hours researching every-thing I had a question about. Things like how to start a business with a blog, what I needed to do to get started, what platforms I was supposed to be on, how to start a digital business, etc. And with each new search answer, I'd think up a hundred more questions to research.

When I wasn't researching, I was marketing. Writing blog posts, putting blogs on my website, setting up my email marketing system, posting on Facebook and Instagram, etc. I was following all of the best practices and recommendations out there and posting to these platforms constantly. Five to six days a week on Instagram and Facebook, and at least two blogs a week.

Then, about eight months in, I created my first digital product - a workbook all about routines. And thanks to my hours of extensive research, I did all of the things you're "supposed" to do when launching.

I spent hours creating it, and then I reached out and got some beta testers. They were sent the workbook, and then once I got their feedback, I spent even more hours re-creating it and improving it based on that feedback.

Finally, I did all of the launch tactics I'd read about. I created an email challenge, designed a sales page, wrote launch emails, and created social media posts around the launch.

I was *certain* that I was going to hit that legendary "successful" tier with this workbook. That I would finally "make it." So sure that I printed out one of those fundraising thermometers and hung it on the fridge - convinced that I would be coloring it in (to the point that I'd need another piece of paper to extend the thermometer) and showing Russell just how worth it his faith in me was. My goal was to hit $1,000 in revenue with that launch.

I made $100.

Now, looking back and knowing what I know now - that launch was actually a huge success. For the price I was selling the workbook for and for the number of people on my email list and in my audience at the time ... my conversion rates were incredible.

Unfortunately, my lack of experience in marketing meant that I had no idea what realistic goals were.

Heck, I didn't even realize that the only thing I'd been doing in my business for the last eight months was marketing. I thought that marketing was what running a business entailed. It turns out it's simply one aspect of running a business.

For most of us in the online business space, we don't have an MBA or business background when we decide to get started. And we probably aren't interested in returning to school to get one. What I want for you is to have the firm foundation that I wish I'd had way back then. So, first, we will talk about what content marketing is, and how to use each type within your marketing plan.

What is Marketing?

Marketing felt overwhelming for many years because I didn't realize what a broad umbrella term it truly was. In my mind, marketing was just marketing, and I was the problem because I didn't "get" it.

Turns out, there are hundreds of different marketing strategies out there, and as technology improves and changes, new ones are created often. Within those hundreds of marketing strategies, we'll spend the majority of this book covering content marketing, as it's a low-cost and simple way for small businesses to market themselves. However, some other marketing strategies would be collaborations, word of mouth, paid ads, and affiliate marketing. In Chapter Five, I'll cover these (and more) in detail and suggest how you can use them in conjunction with your content marketing. It certainly won't be every strategy out there (and, as I said, the strategies are constantly changing and evolving), but it will give you a strong starting point.

So where does content marketing fit into marketing? Let's work from the top down.

Marketing

Organic
Marketing

Content
Marketing

According to Oxford Learner's Dictionary[1], marketing is the action or business of promoting and selling products or services, including market research and advertising.

Basically, anything you do to bring attention to your business? That's marketing.

Within the marketing umbrella, there are two types of marketing - organic and paid marketing. As we're focusing on marketing your business in the most cost-effective way possible, we're going to stick with organic marketing for now and cover paid marketing a bit more in Chapter Five.

So what's organic marketing?

Organic marketing is a subset of marketing that brings attention to your business without paying for utilizing said marketing.

Examples of organic marketing would include:

- Word of Mouth
- Search Engine Optimization
- Content Marketing

And that last bullet point is the star of this book - content marketing. It is a type of marketing that involves the creation and sharing of online material (such as videos, blogs, and social media posts).

Content marketing is a subset of organic marketing. If you're a solopreneur, or you're like I was when I first started and aren't quite sure what you're doing as you get started, it's the ultimate type of marketing in the online business space. It's free to low-cost and has incredible potential for audience and network growth.

The downside to content marketing is that while it's cost-effective, it's not time effective. In the third section of this book, we'll cover how to simplify your content creation process to save time marketing, so you can spend more time working on growing your business.

Within content marketing, there are three types of content that you'll need to create. I often get pushback from clients about not wanting to create certain types of content or not wanting to be on specific platforms. I want to encourage you that you don't need to be everywhere.

However, you also need to remember that when it comes to your business and marketing, it's not about you. In fact, it's never about you. It's all about your audience and what they want from you. So embrace the uncomfortable, and read these next sections with an open mind.

The 3 Types of Content You Need to Create

Long-Form Content

At the time of writing this book, there are three main types of long-form content: blog posts, podcast episodes, and YouTube videos. (Although, as a small business owner, you only need to choose ONE of these to implement.) As time goes on, I'm sure technology will bring us more ways to create long-form content, so what is important to know is that its content that is long enough to go into depth on a topic.

Within your content marketing strategy, the purpose of your long-form content is to nurture your audience and help solve their problems within your pieces of content. You want to send your various audiences on all of your platforms to this one spot where you're putting out your best and most comprehensive content.

Social Media
Channel
Collaborations
Long-Form
Email
Content
Marketing
Interviews

For example, you're going to talk about your long-form content on your social media channels, and you're going to encourage your audience on social media to take the jump over to your piece of long-form content and read/listen/watch. The hope is that they'll enjoy that piece of content so much that they'll come back for the next one, and the one after that. And over time, you can build relationships with your readers/listeners/subscribers with all of the great content you're putting out there for them to enjoy.

The number one question I get from students when we talk about long-form content is - "Is it really necessary?" because long-form content is so time-consuming to create, many business owners prefer to use their social media as their main content platform and create long captions there to showcase their stuff. Here are a few reasons why I wouldn't recommend this:

1. With the exception of YouTube, long-form content is typically hosted in your own space and on land you own. Social media? You don't own it. Your account could be deactivated at any time, and your entire audience? Gone. Just like that. All the hard work you'd have put into growing your audience would be for nothing if you never brought them into your own space.

2. Attention spans get smaller and smaller with each passing year, it seems. And, if you think about your own social media scrolling habits - are you there to learn? Probably not. You're there to be entertained and entertained quickly. If something doesn't hook you from the beginning, you've likely moved on before your brain can even register that you're bored. Long captions that showcase your expertise won't do anything for you if your audience isn't in the right mindset to read and learn.

3. And the dreaded algorithm. As you'll find in Chapter Four, I am very anti-worry about the algorithm. However, it's worth noting here that because there's an algorithm to compete with, your social media content is only going to be shown to a small fraction of the people that follow you. A podcast episode though? 100% of the people that have subscribed are going to get your latest episode delivered right to their phone.

Short-Form Content

Short-form content is, in essence, any social media content you create. Because social media is a rapidly changing area, I won't get into specifics about the different platforms. That would make this book obsolete before I even finished writing it. (*Truly, as I was in the editing phase, a brand new social platform emerged.*)

Here's what I will tell you: don't get too attached to any given type of social media. You've probably seen the rise and fall of a few different platforms at this point. Not to mention that platforms constantly change what they offer and how they work.

This is normal, and that pattern is likely here to stay.

As I'm writing this book, we're in the midst of the rise of a new giant, and fall of another in the social media world. And left and right, I see students, clients, and friends clinging to the old platform, despite how frustrated they are by it. Because they "get" it. Because they prefer it - understandably because that's what they've built their business on. But the data? That's telling a different story. Engagement is down, and the amount of people seeing anyone's content has dropped dramatically. People are spending less and less time on the older platform and more and more on the new one, leading to fewer leads, fewer sales, and lower revenue. In fact, Natalie Franke (co-founder of The Rising Tide Society and small business cheerleader) coined the term "engagement recession" to describe how creators feel about their content's reach on this older platform.

The same thing happened with this older platform when it was the newer platform. Its predecessor began to decline as the new hot platform rolled into town. Is that predecessor still around? Yes, and some people still have success marketing their businesses there. Will this "middle" giant stick around? Most likely, yes. And people will still see success there as well. But is it foolish to ignore the new giant simply because you don't like it or want to learn how to use it? Absolutely.

There's not much that's guaranteed as a business owner, but one thing you can cling to? Change is going to be necessary if you'd like to stick around for the years to come.

See, each social media platform goes through the same life cycle:

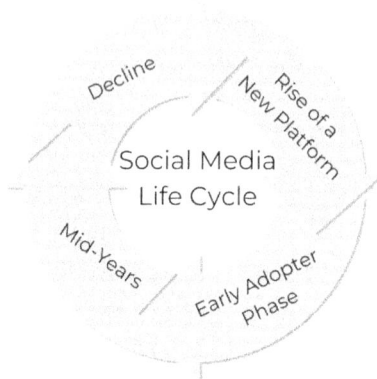

Social Media Life Cycle

Rise of a New Platform

Early Adopter Phase

Mid-Years

Decline

There's not enough information to tell us yet how long each part of the cycle will last, but there are three parts of the cycle that have shown up consistently through the rise and fall of social media platforms.

First, you have the early adopter phase. If possible, this phase is a great time to jump into a new platform. It will sort of be like the Wild West - as in, there are no rules or best practices. This often overwhelms and intimidates business owners, so they stay out. If you can gather the courage to experiment, jumping on a platform at the beginning of its life cycle will help you grow a large audience quickly.

Then, you have the mid-years. It's still possible to see decent growth on the platform, although it's not quite as easy and takes a bit more strategy. Most people will jump in here because there will be educators who put their time and energy into researching what works on the platform and what doesn't. Having guidelines makes it easier, and peer pressure from others jumping on will bring people over. You'll want to focus on growing your audience and building relationships with the audience you already have during this phase.

Finally, the decline. Again, during this phase, it's not going to be impossible to market your business on that platform. However, you're going to want to focus more so on continuing to cultivate relationships with the audience you already have and less on growth. At this point, it tends to be a fight to keep the attention of the audience you have, engagement tends to be down, and it seems like people see less and less of your stuff. So focus on those relationships and move your people to your other types of content.

When it comes to your strategy, the purpose of your short-form content is to build relationships with the audience you have and encourage them to take the next step with you. This can look like a variety of things, but the simplest one is encouraging them to check out your long-form content. Weekly, you should be talking about a piece of long-form content that you've created that they should check out.

Note: I didn't say you had to put out new long-form content each week. Just that you should talk about one of your pieces each week. ☺ We'll chat more about that in Chapter Ten, but I wanted to point that out now.

Another simple way to invite your followers to take the next step? Give them a good reason to get on your email list (like a free download) and share about it weekly.

Email Marketing

Email marketing sort of lives in its own space. Some people will use it as their long-form content if they aren't interested in creating blog posts, podcast episodes, or YouTube videos. This can work if you're feeling too overwhelmed by how much content you need to create. Simply pour that energy into your email newsletter instead.

On the other hand, a common thread among my clients and students is that many don't see the value of emails, especially when they're creating long-form content already. It seems redundant and excessive. However, there are five reasons why I highly encourage an email list (even more than I encourage you to create long-form content):

1. We already discussed the fact that it's important to "own the land" your content is being created on. I've heard of many friends and other creators who have had social media profiles completely disabled, and I've even heard of a large creator whose entire YouTube channel disappeared overnight. All the work you're doing to cultivate your audience would be for nothing if you lost your account and no longer had a way to reach those audience members.

2. A person's email inbox is incredibly personal. Email marketing is the only type of content where your audience member has to invite you in. With all other types of content marketing, the audience member must come to you to receive your content. However, with email marketing, once someone opts in, they've given you permission to come to them. Don't underestimate the power of having the ability to show up in someone's inbox as you choose to.

3. You're in business to make money. Without revenue, your business will not survive. Which means you *have* to be able to effectively sell to your audience. I mentioned earlier that content marketing is cost-effective. This is because the platforms make money the more time people spend on them, which means they want you to create content - for them. They want you to create content so your audience has more to look at and stay on their platform longer. Do you think they're going to make it easy for you to send your people to another platform? Absolutely not. Which makes it hard to sell from any given marketing platform. Email marketing is different in that regard because you're popping right into someone's inbox with emails that include links to exactly what you're selling, making it much easier to convert that email subscriber into a purchaser.

4. Along the same lines, it's easier to sell through email marketing simply because it's less crowded. Most content platforms are noisy. Your content is shuffled off the screen in favor of the next creator's content, and there are suggestions everywhere for other things a user could be looking at. Email inboxes are not the same. Sure, they all get full. But the interface is simple, and once someone reads your email, they aren't distracted by what's next.

They're also reading your email until they choose to move to another, whereas, on some social media platforms, your content will automatically get moved off-screen after a set amount of time.

5. And for those platforms that don't have endless content being served up, you need to consider how we use various platforms. On most platforms, we've been trained to consume as much content as possible. Even if the platform isn't moving people from one piece of content to another, we've become trained to do it ourselves. However, we use email differently. We've been trained that we're in control of our inboxes and that we are responsible for making a choice about each email and how it's used. That may mean we chose to delete an email without opening it, but it still requires the reader to actively make a choice versus mindlessly scrolling. This difference in how we use email is a benefit to email marketers.

Now that we're all on board with utilizing email marketing let's talk strategy. Within your email marketing, there are two subcategories - your sequences and your newsletter, and each has a different purpose.

Email sequences, also known as funnels, are automated emails and tasks that your email subscribers are sent through. Their purpose is twofold: to nurture (build relationships with) your subscribers and to sell to them. Thanks to setting up these sequences, when it's time for your next launch, sale, or offer, you'll have a list full of people in your newsletter list that are nurtured and interested in what you have to offer.

Your email newsletter is your weekly, biweekly, monthly (you choose) email that goes out to your list and nurtures them further by giving them detailed, long-form content. A common question regarding email newsletters is, "What do I talk about"? The simplest way to get started is to tell them about your latest piece of long-form content and encourage them to read/listen/watch. If you're using your email newsletters as your long-form content, then you would create your newsletters based on topics your audience would find interesting or that you know they need more information surrounding what you do.

Where to Show Up

You might be wondering which types of content are right for you. You're interested in starting to create long-form content but aren't sure where. You want to get serious about social media but are overwhelmed by all the platforms. How do you choose?

For long-form content, there are three things you should consider:

1. Your personality type.
2. The amount of time you have for content creation.
3. What your content is about and the best way to present it.

Which Type of Long-Form Content is for You?

BLOG	PODCAST	YOUTUBE
Great for Introverts	Great for Introverts and Extroverts	Great for Extroverts
Least Amount of Time to Create	More Time Consuming than a Blog, but Less than YouTube	Most Amount of Time to Create
Great for Content that Can be Explained by Written Word, or a Graphic/Image	Great for Content that Doesn't Need Visuals	Great for Content that is Best Shown Visually

Are you someone who is more introverted and prefers to be behind the scenes? A blog or a podcast might be the best choice for you.

Are you more extroverted? A podcast or a YouTube channel might be the best bet.

Yes, a podcast is great for both introverts and extroverts, thanks to how customizable it is. For the extreme introverts, you can podcast using only solo episodes that you record by yourself, or you can record guest episodes without cameras. On the other hand, for extreme extroverts, you can podcast mainly with guest episodes and with your camera on, which will give you that joy of interacting with others.

Ask yourself which type calls to you the most. That's the one you'll want to lean into.

However, you'll also want to consider how much time you actually have to create content. YouTube videos will take up much more of your time than a podcast will, and a blog will take up the least amount of time.

Of course, if you're passionate about video but hate writing - in theory, a blog post could take you longer than a Youtube video. You'll also need to consider that when thinking over your available time.

And a final consideration would be the type of content you're going to be creating. If it's heavily visual, you might not want to go the podcast route. However, if it's not that visual, a podcast might be perfect.

There's no right or wrong answer when it comes to which type of long-form content you put out. Ask yourself those three questions, and see where they lead you.

As far as social media goes, there are two things you'll want to consider:

1. Where is your audience?
2. Where do you enjoy showing up?

I know that earlier I said that your marketing isn't about you. And it's not. At the same time, if you're only showing up on one social media platform, it might as well be one you enjoy. Because if you hate it, you won't spend time creating content for that platform, which makes showing up there sort of pointless.

However, I do want you to consider who your audience is and where they're spending their time as well. If you do not want to show up on a certain platform, but it's the best place to reach your audience? You might want to consider a trial run to see if you get more into it than you expect you would.

How do you find your people? Age can play an important role in determining where they might be. Let's face it, various generations use content marketing differently. Again, so as not to age this book prematurely, I won't get into who is where specifically, but considering age should give you a large insight into where your people are.

What Marketing is Not

We've spent quite a bit of time talking about what marketing is - and I could continue to fill books for you on that, but I also want to make sure we touch on what marketing is NOT:

- Sales
- Something to Be Done in a Vacuum
- A Magic Pill

Sales

Does this one surprise you? If it does, you're not alone. It took an embarrassingly long amount of time for this to finally "click" for me. While sales and marketing go hand in hand, they aren't the same thing. **Marketing is the vehicle that brings people to the precipice of a sale, but it's not the sale itself.**

Your content? That is a marketing tool. Your sales page? A sales tool. Your checkout process? A sales tool. Your evergreen funnel emails? All sales tools. Your weekly newsletter? That's a marketing tool. The line is fine, but there is a line between the two. And if you're expecting your marketing to do all the heavy lifting of making the sales happen, you're putting too many expectations on your marketing tools.

Understanding this will also be important for honing in on where things need to improve. For example, if you're wondering why you aren't seeing enough sales, you'll want to look at how many eyes are landing on your sales page and how many sales are happening once people have landed. If you see that 30% of people that land on your sales page are purchasing, you're probably pretty happy with that number, which means your sales process is strong.

On the other hand, maybe that means you're not getting enough people to that sales page. That's a marketing issue, and then you know that you need to share about that offer more in your marketing or vice versa. Understanding that these are separate processes and systems within your business will help you best use your marketing to bring your people to the precipice of that sale and hone in on those sales processes to improve those conversion rates.

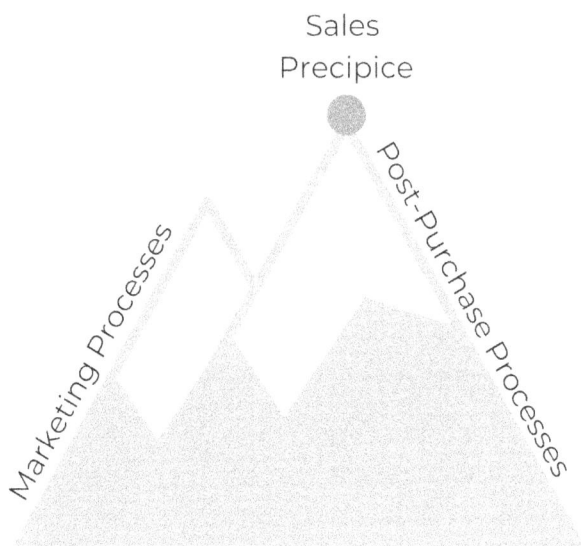

Sales
Precipice

Post-Purchase Processes

Marketing Processes

Something to Be Done in a Vacuum

Another important thing to remember about marketing is that it's not something you can do on your own, especially if you're looking to scale your business. I'll talk more about this in Chapter Five, but for now, it's time to let go of the "if I build it, they will come" mindset and start thinking about the importance of relationships in your marketing. Not only is it important to build relationships with your audience and potential customers, but it's important to build relationships with other business owners in your network because those relationships are going to help you grow your audience faster than you ever could by working in a vacuum.

A Magic Pill

Similar to the ideas above, but one worth turning into its own tiny section, your marketing is not a magic pill to seeing growth as you build a business. Yes, it's an incredibly important part of owning a business. To make sales, you've got to get new eyes on what you're building. And to have a business, you've got to make sales.

However, if you're thinking marketing is going to create sales, and you're attempting to do it all alone - aka creating content, putting it out into the world, and letting that be your entire marketing process - well, you're not going to see much happen. I've worked with too many clients that had incredible gifts to share with the world but ended up folding their businesses after not seeing enough growth. And the problem wasn't their offers, and it wasn't them.

The problem was they thought that all they needed to see growth and build a business was a strong content marketing strategy, and that's the only marketing tool they implemented - and they tried to do it all alone.

My client, Elsie, was a great example of this. We worked together on her content strategy for two years, and each quarter when we hopped on our strategy session call, she was disheartened. I'd come prepared with her data, and those numbers showed growth, albeit slow growth. We would plan ways she could improve the content she was creating, and then we'd strategize each piece of content that she put out so that we were sure it was connecting her audience with her signature offer.

She'd walk away feeling confident and excited, but the next quarter would roll around, and she'd come back disheartened. She wasn't getting in front of enough new people, which meant her revenue wasn't sustainable enough to support her. She was creating content and putting it on her platforms, but she wasn't doing anything outside of that to get in front of new audiences. No matter how awesome your content is or how strategic you're being with it - on its own, your content cannot and will not grow your business because it's simply not a magic pill to success.

In fact, there is no magic pill to success. Growing a business takes time - usually, a lot more time than we expect it to when we first get started. This is why, in Chapter Two, I'm sharing the five permission slips you may need to start marketing without overwhelm.

Action Step:

Choose the platforms you'll be showing up on moving forward. Remember, these aren't permanent and can change in the future, but decide what's reasonable for you for the time being.

Additional Resources:

Chasing Simple Episode 094: What Type of Content is Right for You? *https://amandawarfield.com/094-2/*

For full resources in one place, head to: *https://amandawarfield.com/chasing-simple-marketing-bonuses/*

TWO
YOUR MARKETING PERMISSION SLIP

What I didn't know when I started my business (and creating content) could fill an entire sky with 8-point font writing. We'd all be reading this book *Star Wars* title screen style. And while I certainly would love to have known it all from the beginning, the journey wouldn't have been nearly as sweet to get to where I am. Cliche? Yes. Also true. If I had been able to snap my fingers and have a successful business, I don't think I would have appreciated it nearly as much because I wouldn't have had to pour literal sweat and (many) tears into it.

That being said, there are a few things that I wish I had known from the beginning. If I could go back in time and tell myself, I would. Things that wouldn't take away from the journey, but that definitely would have shortened it a bit. I may not be able to do that for myself, but the least I can do is bestow these pieces of advice to you, my dear friend.

You see, I've talked to business owner after business owner who has a dream or vision for a business, and yet they're spending all of their time taking courses and creating watered-down content because they're scared to own their gifts and talents and say what their dream is. To stand up and say, "My name is _____, and I am a _____."

And the truth is, you'll look back and cringe at the content you create at the beginning. It's not going to be pretty. But if you never get started, you'll never get to where you want to go either. When it comes to getting started, there are five permission slips you may need:

- Don't Force Strategy
- Build Your Own Platform
- Take it One Aspect at a Time
- Be Patient
- Set Realistic Goals

Don't Force Strategy

We will talk extensively about strategy and what I'd recommend your content marketing strategy focus on for each part of your business journey in Chapters Seven, Eight, and Nine. But it's worth noting now because this is the number one thing I wish I could go back and tell myself.

I spent countless hours researching, learning, and trying to understand strategy for content marketing. Hours upon hours feeling like something was missing, without knowing what, and deciding that I needed to re-create my marketing plan to try and fill that hole.

Instead, I wish I had just played around and experimented with my content, but I didn't feel like I could. I felt like experimenting was only reserved for the already successful or the bold. Neither of which I was. And those feelings are a large part of why you have this book in your hand right now. Because I spent so much time and energy trying to "figure out" content marketing and marketing strategy, and not enough time working on other aspects of my business. So, I wanted to create a resource for any entrepreneur in that space. Stuck and overwhelmed by what their content is supposed to be. For the entrepreneurs whose feelings are holding them back from creating growth and momentum in their business because they're spending so much time on marketing. For the entrepreneurs who need permission to experiment and play and understand that growth takes time.

The strategy will come. You don't need to force it from the start.

Build Your Own Platform

The class that made me sweat the most in college was public speaking. I dragged my feet as much as possible to avoid taking that class, and the only thing that made it even halfway bearable was that my professor also loved my favorite TV show - *One Tree Hill* - and was willing to talk about it with me before class began.

The irony is that I now get up on giant stages and speak to rooms full of people for the fun of it.

If you had told sophomore-in-college Amanda that, I would have laughed and then cried because *why?!* What in the world could ever possess me to think that was a good idea?

Weirdly, it turns out that I *love* speaking now. I love teaching and getting on stage to help other entrepreneurs make their content marketing a little bit more simple. There's nothing better than seeing the light bulbs going off over audience members' heads. But the speaking space? It's pretty hard to break into, which is why my speaking coach, Jessica Rasdall, encourages all of us to build our own stage.

What she means by this is that we need to take the time and showcase ourselves as public speakers to show that we are speakers. We could, of course, do this by hosting our own conferences or summits, but her general advice is to start our own content platform that showcases us speaking - aka a podcast or a YouTube channel.

If I could go back to baby business Amanda, I would love to tell her to start Chasing Simple (my podcast) sooner. To not spend so much time blogging and get busy building that stage more quickly. Not only because it would help me to build my own stage as a speaker, but also because it's helped me to build a bridge - one to more and better relationships with other entrepreneurs.

So, even if you have absolutely zero interest in ever doing any kind of speaking, my advice is to at least consider a podcast or YouTube as your long-form content. Is it possible to see success with a blog? Absolutely. But when you have one of these two, you can foster relationships so much more quickly and deeply when you can invite others onto your stage with you. If I could hop in a time machine and let baby business Amanda know that, I would. Since I can't, I hope that I can give you something to think about to shorten the process of building relationships with other business owners.

Take It One Aspect at a Time

Often when we decide there's a new project we want to take on, we go all in. We want to overhaul from top to bottom and do every single part of it just so. But given the fact that content marketing is just one small aspect of our businesses, that's just not realistic. If you decide to go all in to "fix" every part of your content, well, there's a lot to learn.

You could take a course on any number of aspects of your content. Just a few off the top of my head:

- Creating video that engages your viewer
- Capturing pictures and videos that wow
- How to choose hashtags
- Writing captions with SEO
- Strategic content messaging

We could come up with more, but you could potentially purchase a course on all of those topics to "perfect" your content on one platform. However, If you take a moment to think about all the different courses you've bought and how far you've gotten into each of them ... well, I'm sure you can imagine how unlikely, not to mention overwhelming, a scenario that would be.

It's not realistic to expect to overhaul your content in its entirety and make it "perfect". It's also not realistic to expect to learn enough before you get started in order to put out great content from the beginning.

What is realistic is understanding that you're going to start putting out content, and at first, it's not going to be so great, but over time you're going to choose just one small aspect of one type of content to dig into. You'll ask yourself how you can make it better. You'll observe what seems to be working for other creators. And yes, maybe you'll even buy and take a course on it. But you'll improve one thing and then choose another to improve. And so on and so forth until you feel confident about your marketing.

Be Patient

As a business owner, patience will be a much-practiced and incredibly necessary skill. This is something I struggle with weekly, even six years in. But the first year or two? My patience was at an all-time low. I expected my business to grow so much faster than it did, and I was constantly overwhelmed and annoyed by the slow growth I saw.

Until one day when I was driving home from my teaching job and soaking up a business podcast as I drove home. As usual, the host asked her guest how she got started in her business. As usual, the guest began to share the journey she experienced to get to where she was. As usual, she started talking about how she'd run a blog for a few years before turning it into a business, and wow! Within the first year, she'd hit six figures! Isn't that just amazing?

What wasn't usual was that I had an epiphany at that moment.

All around me, it seemed, I'd see content or content creators that hinted at, or even outright said, they hit six figures in their first year in business. And I was sitting there, working my butt off to make $100 in my first year. I felt so defeated. What was I doing wrong? Why wasn't I seeing *any* traction? How is it possible that I was working so much only to see 0.1% of the success they did?

And at that moment, listening to that podcast, I realized - these success stories of hitting six figures in one year? They almost *always* came right after the words**, "I've been writing a blog for years."**

For *years*, these business owners had been creating content and growing and building an audience. So, of course, when it came time to sell, they had people to sell to. And that's no shade to these business owners. I know they worked their booty off for those years and beyond, creating content and building those audiences. I know they worked hard and had to be strategic and intentional to hit those six figures even after years of growing an audience.

But understanding that while it might have been their first year in business, **it wasn't their first year marketing themselves** - that light bulb moment made all of the difference for me and how I felt about my business, and myself as a business owner.

And I want *you* to understand that as well. Because if you are jumping into the online business world with no audience, no network, and no MBA, you will have to take time to build an audience. Without an audience, there's no one to sell to. Have patience with yourself. It takes time. It takes more time than you think it will. But you aren't the problem. Your content isn't the problem. Give yourself plenty of grace and patience as you focus on getting started and hoping to see growth.

Set Realistic Goals

There are about a million more things I've learned along the way and wish I knew way back when I was first getting started, but I'll leave you with one final "If I could go back in time" lesson. I wish I knew how to set realistic goals. As a launch strategist, this lesson is one of the most heartbreaking to watch play out.

I wish the girl who spent an hour in Canva creating a thermometer printable and hung it on the freezer door with the number "$1,000!" written on top of it had known how to set realistic goals. I wish she knew she should have been writing "$100!" and still would have been going above and beyond. I wish she knew that "build it and they will come" does NOT work, and that just because something exists, that doesn't mean that the people who would want and need it will magically find it.

I wish I had known that business, and marketing, are all about relationships. But it's also a numbers game. I'll walk you through the math in just a moment, but you can take the number of people on your email list, multiply it by 1%, and then multiply it by 2%, and you'll have yourself a range of what you can reasonably expect to see sales-wise during a launch or promotion. I wish I had known that those seven sales with less than 100 people on my email list were outrageous and should have been above and beyond my expectations for that launch.

It certainly would have saved me a lot of heartache to know all of that.

But now you do. So next time you plan to host a sale or promotion, and you're setting your goals for revenue or the number of sales, use hard numbers to see what you can realistically expect before you set unrealistic expectations and put more pressure on yourself than necessary.

Let's Do the Math

At the time of writing this, the industry standard for the online business space is 1-2%[2]. If you have an engaged audience, or you know you've done a really good job of bringing in warm leads, you can bump those numbers up to 5-10% to set your goals.

So, 1,000 people on your list means you can expect 10 - 20 sales according to the industry average.

1000 X .01 = 10

1000 X .02 = 20

Or, if you have 1,000 people on your list, but you know you've done a darn good job of building relationships with your audience, you might be able to reach 50 - 100 sales.

1000 X .05 = 50

$$1000 \times .10 = 100$$

Now, if you've got 1,000 people on your list, and you're selling a $47 product, the industry average says that you'll make somewhere between $470 and $940.

$$1000 \times .01 = 10 \times 47 = \$470$$

$$1000 \times .02 = 20 \times 47 = \$940$$

However, if you've focused on relationship building and not growth for the sake of growth, you're more likely to see somewhere in the $2,350 - $4,700 range.

$$1000 \times .05 = 50 \times 47 = \$2,350$$

$$1000 \times .10 = 100 \times 47 = \$4,700$$

That's a huge difference. And I've seen this play out in my own business. At the beginning of 2021, I had just 300 people on my email list. But a full third of those people were students inside of my course, Content Batching Bootcamp. And with just 300 people on my email list, I was able to leave my teaching job for good. The numbers don't matter as much as the relationships do.

Even better than using industry averages for your goals, though, is if you've run a launch or promotion previously. Then, you'll have your averages to set even more realistic expectations. Again, these numbers aren't guaranteed, and in business, there are always surprises, but it's a lot more helpful than just pulling a number out of thin air that you'd like to make and hoping and praying that it happens.

Now that you've gotten your crash course in marketing and have an idea of how to get started, there's one more extremely important part of marketing that we have to talk about before we can talk about strategy and messaging. Relationship building - like how my speech teacher brought me to class with our *One Tree Hill* bonding. You'll see throughout the book that relationships are a key foundation piece of owning and running a successful business, and we want to make sure cultivating relationships with our audience is baked into all of our content marketing.

Action Step:

Give yourself permission to start without understanding everything. Truly, take a piece of paper and write, "I can serve others right where I am," and then post it somewhere you'll see it. You don't have to have everything figured out to serve your people well.

Additional Resources:

Chasing Simple Episode 040: Implement a Content Strategy that Converts
https://amandawarfield.com/040-2/

For full resources in one place, head to:
https://amandawarfield.com/chasing-simple-marketing-bonuses/

THREE
BUILD IT AND THEY WON'T COME

As a new business owner, I fell into the belief and mindset of "build it, and they will come." I thought if I put out content that would help someone, they would find it. If I created a great offer, the people who needed it and could use it would find it.

Looking back, I'm not sure what made me fall into this thinking. Maybe it was a lack of understanding of how search engine optimization worked - I mean, I always found what I needed on the internet. So surely, everyone who needs my stuff will find it too. Maybe it was because I was consuming so much information on how to create content worth consuming that I drove right by the exit that told me I needed to get people to it, also. Maybe it was a general naivety. Maybe it had to do with the way business-starting-gurus market their courses as "all you need to get started" but then go on to only tell you how to set up the foundations and that marketing your new business is just creating content for your audience. Maybe a combination of all of the above.

In case you're falling into the same trap, let me be clear: no matter how incredible your content or your offer is, people are not going to just find you. It takes intention to get the right people in front of your content. (Which we will discuss in-depth in Chapters Five through Nine, don't you worry.) Once you get them there, you've got to give them a reason to stick around. Creating quality content is only the beginning. You also need relationships with your audience members.

Relationship Marketing

It was my first day of work, and I was meeting my coworkers. There was one guy that was kind of cute, so I thought, "Eh, he'll do." By the end of our shift, I invited him to my house to hang out, and he accepted.

Once we got there, we spent hours talking. Everything from how his day had gone, to what his interests were, to what mine were, to the weather, and the upcoming holiday ... I mean, we covered every option.

After exhausting all of the conversation options, I felt like our relationship was built up enough to start a little flirting. So, I pulled out all of my flirty options. I even did a few of them multiple times. Especially asking about his love life. I love using that one.

Once he got flirty back, I stepped up my game, and we had our very first kiss. Which quickly turned into more, and I'll spare you all the details, but by the end of the night he'd moved in, and we were eloping in my kitchen.

Thus goes every single scenario that I ever play in The Sims.

And that's the only time a relationship ever works like that. In reality, my relationship with my husband started with us playing Words With Friends back and forth for weeks without anyone saying anything other than "good game" (even though I was absolutely terrible and there was no way Russell was enjoying the gameplay).

The question is, how do you build relationships with your audience members? I once saw a marketing expert say that you had to put calls to action at the end of every single piece of content in order to get engagement from your audience. And while they weren't wrong ... it's not quite so simple. We don't want engagement for the sake of engagement. We don't want engagement from bots or disingenuous engagement from someone trying to game the system and cold message others. We want genuine engagement. And to encourage genuine engagement, you need to lean into relationship marketing.

Relationship marketing is less a type of marketing and more a focus of your marketing. That focus is genuine relationships. I won't get up on my soapbox about genuine relationships versus trying to build relationships to get ahead, but I will give this one tiny reminder - if you aren't genuinely interested in building relation-ships with your audience - it shows.

And as one more reminder - this is a long-term strategy. This is not something you can force overnight like you can't force marriage in a day (unless you're playing The Sims).

So how do you do it? With three important factors:

- Consistency
- Know, Like, and Trust
- Community

Consistency

Last summer, I had an incident of food poisoning, and right before it began, I noticed something was wrong. I felt my heart racing even though all we were doing was lying on the couch, watching *Iron*

Man 2. I checked my watch, and my heart rate was up to 130. Within minutes, I became very sick. I immediately felt better, and my heart rate calmed back down, but that moment when it started racing had me checking my heart rate at all times. I'd never particularly cared before, but that moment was scary enough to make me curious.

And within a few days, I'd decided that I needed to finally get serious about working out and taking care of my heart. You see, as a kid, I was always active and involved in sports. Not sporty, mind you. I was actively terrible, thanks to my incredibly low hand-eye coordination abilities, but I was involved. In high school, I went to the gym with my dad almost daily. And I never really had to think about being active and working out because it was a natural rhythm.

Then I went to college. Even though I was walking all over campus, my workouts fell off hard about halfway through the first semester. There was just always so much going on, and my dorm was on the literal opposite side of campus from the gym. Walking all the way there, working out (solo - which 18-year-old Amanda did not possess the confidence to do, I'm sad to say), walking back, showering ... it was just too much. And ever since then, working out has been a chore. Something I hated and actively dreaded.

But last summer, I was determined to start taking better care of myself and to get back into it. After years of inconsistency, that fear for my heart was enough to jump-start me into building a routine. For the next year, I worked solely on being consistent. Solely on showing up in the garage with my husband three times a week.

And for a year, I didn't see any progress. Truthfully, it was frustrating. It felt so slow and was a true test of patience. After an entire year of working on being consistent in working out and moving my body, I wasn't losing any weight. At least that the scale showed or that I could visibly see.

But - under the surface, my body was changing. I couldn't see it, and the scale wasn't showing it, but slowly muscle was being formed and slowly replacing the fat. It took time, patience, and consistency to get to a place where enough fat was depleted to see those muscles underneath that I'd been building.

It was just the other week - over a year into consistently working out - that I began to look in the mirror and see toned lines and muscles barely peeking out on my arms and thighs. And there's still plenty more progress to be made. And I trust that it will, over time, thanks to consistency.

Does consistency mean perfection? Absolutely not. When we first started working out, I wasn't worried about improving what I was eating, how long or intense the workouts were, or even making sure I was rotating through different workouts to evenly work all my muscles and including weights, stretching, cardio ... All of those things are important for health gains. But I didn't have the capacity to focus on each of them. All I could handle was making sure I got into the gym consistently. It wasn't perfect. It was messy. But results did come through in time.

Ever since I began to teach the importance of consistency with content creation, I've realized that consistency is key no matter what our goals are in life. If you're looking to see progress in taking care of yourself? Consistency. Looking to learn a new skill? Consistency. Looking to market your business? Consistency. You must consistently show up to build those foundations for your goals.

We'll discuss consistency in depth in Chapter Ten. But, for now, know that consistency is a key part of building relationships with your audience.

Know, Like, and Trust

The Know, Like, and Trust Factor is another key to building relationships with your audience. These are three stages that we go through to establish and build a relationship with someone else. Think about when you start a friendship with someone new. First, you come to know them. Then you start to like them. And finally, you trust them.

Stage One   Stage Two   Stage Three

Know   Like   Trust

You wouldn't tell a new acquaintance your deepest secret the day you meet, would you? No. Because you don't trust them yet.

When it comes to marketing, it's no different. The goal with your marketing is to have your audience get to know you, decide if they like you, and then decide if they trust you and believe in you and your business. If they do, they'll become a customer. If they don't, they'll either be on their way or stick around until they decide to trust you.

So how do you build this Know, Like, and Trust factor?

You've got to let your audience get to know you. A large part of that comes from showing up consistently. Not only by the belief that they can trust you but also just by the nature of being in their feed or inbox or earbuds once again. The more you show up, the more they come to know you. But there are also four things you can do to help build that Know, Like, and Trust factor in your content:

- Building a Personal Brand
- Being Vulnerable
- Engaging Back
- Core Values

Building a Personal Brand

Outside of showing up consistently, building a brand is important. Now, the easiest way to do this is by building a personal brand. That makes you the face of your company, and people come to get to know you, as well as your business. This tends to come easier because we relate better to individual humans than we do a brand since we can begin to think of them as friends. You may love Disney, but you wouldn't think of it as your friend, right? But Taylor Swift? If you're a Swiftie, you, without a doubt, believe you and Taylor could be best friends if you met "IRL."

Here's my word of caution, though - it can be easy to lose yourself in becoming a personal brand. At some point, it's easy to lose the thread of where you end and where your business begins. Boundaries will be important and necessary, and please remember that you don't owe anyone anything about your life.

There are five things my audience knows about me: 1) I'm obsessed with my cats. 2) I spend as much time as possible with my husband. 3) I'll try and fit Disney into every conversation. 4) I spend entirely too much time invested in University of South Carolina sports (Go Gamecocks!), and 5) I read a lot. All of these things are very real parts of who I am. And because they're very real parts of who I am, they've naturally slipped into my content over time.

When I first started, I picked one thing about myself to share to make my content feel more human, and that was the cats. If you asked an audience member to tell you something about me, it would probably be about the cats. They've always been along for the ride. As you evolve into a personal brand, pick one thing you love that you could talk about forever. For now, don't worry about how you will "fit it" into your content. That'll come with time if you pick something you can spend hours talking about.

Building a personal brand is the fastest way to build that Know, Like, and Trust factor. However, if you are not interested in a personal brand, your business isn't a lost cause. You have to build a brand around your business. Now, I'm not a brand expert but look to the businesses you see around you that have great brands without being a personal brand.

The first one that comes to mind for me is Duolingo.

Now, I have never once used Duolingo. I haven't even considered it. I didn't even know what the app was until its content started showing up in my social media feed. But they've done a great job of using their brand to bring awareness to the business.

If you haven't seen their content, they have an owl mascot named Duo. This owl is part of their branding, and they went and bought a costume for an employee to wear in their content. (And I'm sure they have other uses for it, but like I said, I only know this business because of their social media content.)

And their content has become known for being silly, snarky, and almost but not quite, provocative. (Or, as provocative as you can get when the main feature of your content is a giant owl costume.)

Another example would be the Empire State Building. Yes, that one. There is an entire official Empire State Building social media account that was created to build a brand around the Empire State

Building. And the vast majority of the content is images of the building, or "Point of View" from the building with references to current pop culture events and happenings.

In both scenarios, creating connection points works best for drawing people in. Which, again, isn't dissimilar to "real life" interactions and relationships. And the bottom line of each piece of content is connecting with other people who'll "get it."

Being Vulnerable

You'll also want to "let your audience in." By this, I mean don't just show them the front-facing parts of your business. Open the door and show them behind the scenes. This could mean everything from simply showing what you're working on any given day, or a fun thing you did over the weekend, all the way to sharing about hard things you're struggling with. By opening the door up and showing them what's behind your expertise, it helps them envision you in other parts of life.

When it comes to being vulnerable, choosing what to share and what not to within your content is a personal journey. For example, I'm pretty open about my health issues with Glaucoma and Endometriosis, but you aren't going to see me sharing about fights that my husband and I might have. Or family issues that are happening behind the scenes. And not because I'm necessarily trying to hide anything, but there are just some conversations I can't add to. For me, speaking up about my Glaucoma and Endometriosis might help another person, and that's something I'm passionate about because of the way my diagnoses have come about. Could me sharing how Russell and I resolve disagreements help someone else? Probably. But it's not something that I feel passionate about, and it's not a conversation I feel like I can necessarily add much to. The difference between these two scenarios is a slim line, which is why it's such a personal journey.

Engaging Back

Next, you'll want to make sure you're engaging back. This one is important. You don't want to create content and throw it into the void.

In Chapter Four, we'll talk about marketing practices you can discard and one of those is going to be cold messaging and engagement. I want to preface that section now that what I'm talking about here is not what I'm talking about there. Welcome to the world of business - where everything is shades of gray and has a fine line. (Which is why you must question everything in marketing. Everything.)

What I don't want you to do is sit there and engage because someone told you to engage for a certain amount of time, or that you have to engage right before and after posting something, or any other rule that might be out there about engaging that you're tempted to do to simply check it off your to-do list.

What I do want you to do is take time to notice who is engaging with your content. If there's someone whose username is popping up over and over again, head over to their content and interact with it as well. Try and find something you have in common. Start a DM with them. Not because you want to sell to them. And not because you're being spammy. But because they've made overtures towards friendship towards you, it's time to make them back.

Core Values

Growing up, I always wanted to be a teacher. So back in the spring of 2018, when I first started my business, I was teaching preschool. And I loved it. But I also wanted more for myself. One of the biggest struggles in our marriage was the lack of quality time. Of course, Russell's work schedule was the majority of the problem because he was in the military, and when you're in the military, they tell you when to work and for how long. There's very little time off. But my work schedule often got in the way when he did have time off.

I started dreaming about the better life we could have if I ran my own business and could make my own hours, and it sounded so appealing. I thought that, surely, I'd be making six figures within the first year. I could walk away from teaching and have a much more flexible schedule. I not only thought it was possible but feasible. Because that's what the marketing around me seemed to be screaming. "Use this product to hit six figures!" "Buy my templates and be on your way to six figures!"

It seemed like that's what everyone was making, so I figured, why not me too?

And, not so surprisingly, that didn't happen. The 2018-2019 school year began, and I hadn't made any money yet. But I figured, hey, just one more year of teaching. By the end of this school year, I'll be ready to quit.

And at the end of that school year, I quit teaching. But it wasn't because I was successful. I'd made a whopping $1,100 in total from the business by that point. And that's revenue. Not profit.

Russell's contract was up with the Navy, and we were moving back home. Because of the timing of the move, I wasn't going to be able to find a teaching job for that school year, so we agreed that I would go full-time in my own business for one school year while we were getting settled, and if I hadn't shown some traction towards replacing my income, then I would need to get another teaching job.

And I worked my ass off to try and make it happen. Ridiculous hours. Ridiculous amounts of stress. So much so that Russell and I were fighting often about it because I was seeing no revenue growth while also letting it take over my life.

Everywhere I turned, it seemed that everyone else had so much success, and I began to think that I was the problem. I should have hit six figures already and blown past it, and because I hadn't, it must be me. I must not be cut out for entrepreneurship.

I felt like such a failure. But I also couldn't seem to give up. I picked up a couple of very part-time jobs to bring in a tiny bit of income to supplement what I wasn't making. Russell was beginning to bring up conversations about me needing to look for a teaching job because there still hadn't been any growth in the business in the five months since we'd moved back.

And then, March 2020 rolled around. This put off the talk of finding a job for the new school year because no one knew what the next school year would bring. (We didn't even know what the next day would bring!) And that April, I finally started to see some traction. I got a couple of clients. I finally was starting to understand my messaging. And then, I uncovered what would ultimately become my signature offer - teaching how to batch content.

From that point forward, I started to see continuous growth. But let me be clear - continuous growth does not mean six-figure success. I was seeing just enough growth to show Russell and myself that this was going to work. Still, to this day, I have not made six figures in my business. I've replaced my income, and my revenue gets higher each year. But it's not what others might call success.

y1: $109 >> y2: $1,085 >>

y3: $13,804 >> y4: $27,452 >>

y5: $44,696 >> y6: ??

In my first year of business, I made just around $100. In year two? Just over $1,000. An 895% increase in revenue. Which sounds great, but $1,000 in revenue can't sustain a business. Then in year three, I made almost $14,000. A 1,172% increase from the year before. This is when things finally started to feel realistic. I still wasn't replacing my income, but I could see it happening. The next year? About $27,400 in revenue. A 98% increase in revenue. I'd finally replaced what I would have made teaching preschool. The year after that? A 63% increase in revenue brought me to a little under $45,000. And this year? I'm on track to hit $60,000 in revenue, which would be about a 34% increase from last year.

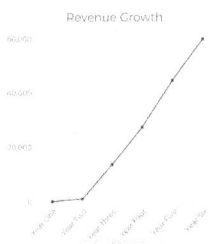

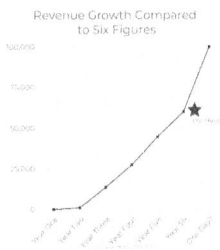

Revenue Growth

Revenue Growth Compared to Six Figures

Maybe you're reading this, and you can't believe I'm sharing my actual numbers with you. But something I'm passionate about is not leading anyone astray or making it seem as if I'm more successful than I am. I'm very open about my numbers. I'm very honest with how my launches go and what those numbers look like. And I'm very open about the things that I struggle with as an entrepreneur. Basically, I try to be open and honest to the point that might be detrimental.

Is there a risk and a fear that when I'm open like that, my audience will look at my content and think, "She's not my version of success-ful, so she's not worth learning from"? Absolutely. It's terrifying. But what's even more terrifying to me is the idea that I'm contributing to someone else's anxiety and feelings of failure by putting on a front that says, "Hey! Look at me! Buy from me! Learn from me! I know exactly what to do, and I'm very successful!"

I'm sure there are plenty of people out there that have listened to my podcast or read my content and decided I wasn't worth learning from because I wasn't that big successful six or seven-figure entrepreneur. But there are also thousands of people who have seen my vulnerability and decided to stick around. And those are my people, and the community I've intentionally built is one around vulnerability in entrepreneurship.

In my case, my clients and students stick around because they know I'll be honest and open with them and that vulnerability is a core value that I hold for my business. That core value is something my audience aligns with, so they stick around. Vulnerability may not be a core value for you and your business, and that's okay. But take some time to think about what your core values are because those core values are connection points that you can make with your audience to build the Know, Like, and Trust factor.

How do you determine your core values? These are one of those things that are going to evolve naturally over time and are not something you want to force - similar to content strategy and messaging. However, two places you can find inspiration for those core values are your main mission statement (why you started your business and what you're hoping to achieve with it) and your values as a business owner.

What's important to you? What motivates you to succeed? What principles mean something to you? Your personal values won't always be your business core values, but there often is overlap, or at the very least, your personal values are often the foundation on which you build your business values.

Give yourself permission not to have these figured out right away, but once you do determine yours, core values are important for building the Know, Like, and Trust factor and often are a strong starting point for building community in your business.

Community

Community (noun): A feeling of fellowship with others as a result of sharing common attitudes, interests, and goals.[3]

Over time, as you build relationships with your audience, you'll find that you're attracting people that could benefit from knowing each other. If they align with your core values, that means that they have similar core values with each other as well, right?

As humans, we are social beings that thrive in community with others. It fulfills those basic needs of connection, belonging, and support. When you're going through hard things, having community means that you aren't alone. You've got others willing to listen to you and who you're walking that journey with.

You might be thinking something along the lines of "But Amanda. I run a sticker shop. What in the world would a community about stickers do for someone?" I want to remind you to refer back to that last section on core values. On the surface, your community might be there as a place to share planner spreads with each other, but at a deeper level - why do you love stickers? Why does your audience love stickers? What could having a community of other people that feel the same way do for someone?

Maybe you have a core value of self-expression, and the stickers in your planner are simply one way that you go about encouraging your self-expression. So, you create bold and beautiful stickers. If your audience members have similar core values and love infusing their day-to-day with bright, bold visuals, they would be an excellent fit for your community. Maybe they're surrounded in their "real life" by people who don't get their love of self-expression. Maybe they're seen as the "bold" friend. But in your community? They're just one of many, and that feeling of belonging helps bring peace and confidence into the other aspects of their life where this part of them may stick out.

Creating community means giving a place for your people to gather and find their people, too. It creates a space where what you're doing with your business is bigger than just you. Being in a community with others that value the same things as you gives you a feeling of belonging. No matter how old you get, having that in your life is important.

Business Benefits to Building Community

If building a community for the sake of helping others enjoy those benefits of community isn't enough, there are also business benefits of creating a community for your people.

INCREASED BRAD REPUTATION AND LOYALTY. When someone feels like they belong inside of a community you've created, those good feelings are going to fall onto you as well. That connection they feel means they're more likely to stay loyal to the brand and continue to show up again and again.

ANOTHER AVENUE FOR SELLING. Creating a community gives you another place to talk about your offers and promotions and makes your biggest fans more likely to see your posts about your promotions at any given time. On top of that, because your biggest fans are inside of your community, they're likely going to be doing the selling for you simply by talking about what they love about your offers. That social proof will do more for your sales than any promotion you put together.

SIMPLER MARKET RESEARCH. Every post and comment that an audience member leaves inside of your community is a chance to better understand your audience's needs. By paying attention to the questions and comments left in the community, you can better hone in on your content messaging and topics to better serve your people.

How to Build Community

Now that you're convinced that building a community is an important part of strong relationships with your audience, where do you begin? First, you'll want to identify your audience and the group's purpose. It's okay if this is wide initially, but you'll want to narrow it down as much as possible. "Mini Session Tips for Family Photographers" will bring in more people than "Photography Tips" simply because of clarity.

Next, you'll need to choose a platform. Whether you use a social media platform, a forum, a messaging app, or some other group of your creation, you'll need a place for your community to gather virtually.

Then, you've got to create valuable content. You've got to give people a good reason to join the community, so be sure to be ready to create content that your people will get value from. Hosting special "events" just for your community and having exclusive content for them is also a huge benefit. Things like going live, hosting calls just for them, creating a special challenge, etc., are all great ways to do this.

Finally, cultivate your community. Make sure you're engaging with your people and also encouraging them to engage with each other. Your audience members are the center point of your community, not you. Having them build relationships with each other is just as important, if not more so, than building relationships with you.

Relationship Building in Practice

A lot of the information in this chapter might feel a bit elusive because building relationships, especially in a digital world, is such a personal journey for each entrepreneur. Because each of us is so different, and our audiences are all so different, it's impossible to write in a way that will very specifically help you as the reader and also the next reader and the next. The way that you specifically gather community and what you say to build Know, Like, and Trust is going to vary from person to person. But I always love actionable steps, so I wanted to add a final section to this chapter that will give you ideas for your content so you can intentionally leverage that to build relationships with your audience.

First, we've got tutorial posts. In these, you're giving step-by-step guidance on how to do something you're an expert on. You're providing value and serving your audience by doing so. In return, they're more likely to come back for more of that great content, but also they'll start to see you as the expert you are.

Some examples of tutorial content would be:

- "X Ways to [Do a Thing]"
- "X Steps to [Achieve an Outcome]"
- "Next Time You Want [This] - Do [This One Thing]"
- Give tips to your audience on a topic

Then, we've got personal posts. These are great for building your personal brand and making connections with your audience. Examples would be:

- Introduction posts
- Posts about things you love and that make you, you
- Behind-the-scenes content

Finally, there are problem-centric posts. Here you're going to focus on the problems that your audience is facing and how you can help them. Examples of these would be:

- Sharing a story of when you struggled with the same problem
- Sharing a story about a client of yours that struggled with the same problem
- Sharing something they need to know about something they struggle with

And remember - a key part of relationship building is inviting your audience further by including a call to action. As I mentioned earlier, it's not enough in and of itself to build community. But it is an important piece of your content strategy. And then, be sure to respond. If they take that next step, meet them there. If you ask them to leave a comment, reply to their comment. If you ask them to share and you see them sharing, thank them for doing so. If you ask them to send you a message, make sure you reply. A call to action isn't going to magically make people engage, but once they feel ready to, it'll give them clear next steps on how to do so. You've just got to build that relationship foundation and then continue that relationship yourself.

Now that you know where to begin with your marketing, let's talk about how *not* to go about getting started. In the next chapter, we'll be discussing marketing practices you can mark off of your to-do list now.

Action Step:

Take some time and free-flow journal out your thoughts around your business mission (who you want to help and how) and your personal values. If you have any thoughts as to what your business core values might be, journal those too. If not, no big deal - remember that it's okay to let those evolve over time.

Additional Resources:

Chasing Simple Episode 104: 9 Posts that Build Relationships with Your Audience?
https://amandawarfield.com/104-2/

For full resources in one place, head to:
https://amandawarfield.com/chasing-simple-marketing-bonuses/

FOUR
MARKETING PRACTICES TO DISCARD

Earlier, I shared the epiphany I had while listening to a podcast where I realized that many of the overnight six-figure business owners had been building audiences to sell to for years before "starting" their businesses. This helped me realize that what was seemingly happening overnight actually wasn't, and this was one of the hardest mindset shifts I've had to make as a business owner. That growth takes time and a lot of it. You've already heard about my initial grand visions of making six figures in my first year and where I am six years later.

The second hardest mindset shift? That the "rules" really don't matter with your content.

When I first started, I spent hours and hours researching and learning how to make my content successful. I scoured podcasts, blogs, and free downloads, trying to learn all the secrets to content that will skyrocket a business.

As a One on the Enneagram, I love nothing more than to follow the rules. If you aren't an Enneagram follower, it is a personality typing system, and Ones are known as "perfectionists". They love order and rules and doing this "right." So, when someone gives me a "supposed to," I do it.

When educators said to do everything I could to make the algorithm happy, I spent hours figuring out what the algorithm even wanted.

When they said to get on and engage for 15 minutes every time I post, I did that.

When they said to comment on ten different people's posts and stories each day, I tried that.

I tried just about everything "experts" said about pleasing the algorithm and seeing growth and spoiler alert - none of it worked.

Eventually, I hit a wall.

All that work and all that time weren't getting me anywhere.

I began to focus solely on creating good content. On interacting with the people that were interacting with me. In cheering on those I'd love to connect with or meet at some point.

And it felt like a door had opened, revealing a sunny, grassy meadow, and I could finally just *enjoy* my content.

This is how I want content marketing to feel for you as well, and that means we'll need to remove what's blocking the door - growth practices that aren't worth your time. There are four common practices that I see business owners using to try to grow their content channels that you can say goodbye to:

- Pleasing the Algorithm
- Cold Messaging
- Bots

- Trends

Pleasing the Algorithm

The first practice to say goodbye to is shifting your plan to accommodate what the algorithm supposedly wants at any given time. Frankly, the algorithm doesn't seem to know what the algorithm wants most of the time, and it's not worth your time to worry about it either.

On top of that, the algorithm was created to allow the platform to personalize the content that you're seeing so that they could keep you interested and on their platform, which raises retention rates and advertising revenue. Basically? The algorithm is there to help the platform make money. It wasn't created to help you get your content seen.

Your content marketing is only a small part of your business, and if you're spending time focusing on what the algorithm wants, you're NOT spending time on revenue-generating activities. These are activities that will actively bring in more money for you. For example, improving your offers, collaborating with others, or creating content for your content platforms where you don't need to fight the algorithm and can sell much easier.

A few years ago, there was a rumor that a certain social media platform would knock your content if you used a scheduling tool, which led to a frenzy of people refusing to use scheduling tools and only ever posting in real time. To them, it was just a quick minute to find the content they'd created, copy/paste it into the app and hit publish.

In reality, when it comes to taking the time for a task, we often tell ourselves that it will only take a minute or two here and there, and it's okay, we can spare it. Over time, those one to two minutes add up. And are often longer than the one to two minutes we think they are. Plus, these creators were probably trying to post according to their "best" time for peak engagement, so when that time came, they would have to stop everything they were doing, go find the content they'd already created, and then publish it. On top of that, how many times have you ever gone onto a social media app to publish something and *didn't* get distracted and start scrolling?

Not to mention, once they finally got off the app, they'd have to get back into the groove of the task they were doing before, which is no easy feat. According to a study by Dr. Gloria Mark with the University of California Irvine[4], it takes on average, twenty-three minutes and fifteen seconds to get back into a task post-distraction. So all of a sudden, that one to two-minute task to post in real-time? It's actually taking thirty minutes, forty-five minutes, or even an entire hour to do each day.

If you posted five days a week, that's about twenty hours a month that you're devoting just to *posting* your content. Not to mention creating it. Each month you'd be spending half of a work week just to post on social media, all in the name of making the algorithm happy.

To take it a step further, consider how much money you could have made if you spent those twenty hours serving clients. If your hourly rate is $50, twenty hours of work is $1,000 a month you'd miss out on. $1,000 a month? That's $12,000 a year. Imagine what your bottom line could have looked like if you had an extra $12,000 on it last year.

The worst part? This rumor? Totally bogus. This app even has its own scheduling tool. Why would they spend the time and money building that out if they were just going to discourage you from using it? Rumors about what the algorithm prefers aren't worth your time.

Even if it had been true, spending that much time trying to make the algorithm happy isn't where you should be spending your time. Instead of focusing on what the algorithm may or may not want, tune in to your own practices as you're consuming any given type of content. Slowing down and thinking through what I'm naturally doing has given me more insight into better practices than anything else.

For example, as social media apps shift and change in order to keep people interested and on the app longer, I pay attention to how I'm using new features. If I find that I'm consuming less of a certain type of content and more of another, I'll shift my content plan so that I'm creating less of the one I'm consuming less and more of the one I'm consuming more of. It's not a foolproof plan, but it's been very helpful in knowing where to focus my attention and where not to on apps that are continuously getting crowded with new features.

Cold Messaging

The slimiest of the slimy, this practice often comes from trying to hit targets such as "connect with ten new people a day," and the hope is to see growth by getting in front of more people. This practice involves leaving comments on other people's content, sending direct messages, interacting with multiple pieces of content all at the same time, and so on. The purpose is to gain attention, and the hope is that these people will click over to your profile, like what they see, and decide to give you a follow.

Will it work? Occasionally. But usually not, which is why it's referred to as "casting a wide net." You get in front of ten new people a day, fifty a week, and at some point, a few will follow back (aka not slip through the holes in your net).

There are a couple of problems with this idea, though. First, I'll just refer you right back up to the time theory in the last section. You're spending an exorbitant amount of time hoping to see growth instead of working on revenue-generating activities. You've got to find those ten new people each day, which takes time. Then you've got to look through their content and try to find something to comment on or interact with. Then you've got to create the comment. And then you must find nine more people to do that to. Every. Single. Day. On top of that, a follow does not guarantee revenue growth.

Second, most of us can see right through these tactics. They range from someone liking a ton of your posts, to leaving a few comments, to sending a direct message, but the intention is *always* clear once you've been around the social media space for long enough. Heck, some people even just jump straight into the pitch in message one. But even for those that don't - no matter how authentic you think you're coming off, we can see whether a message or comment is genuine and if the intention is interaction for interaction's sake.

The fact of the matter is that even if you genuinely want to connect with people using this method, if you're using this practice, there's nothing genuine about your connections. It all comes down to the base motivation behind why you're commenting or interacting with someone's content. If you go into connecting with a goal in mind of connecting with X amount of people, and you're trying to find new people to connect with, it will be screamingly obvious in those messages/comments/etc.

It may seem like I'm splitting hairs here, but the heart of why you're interacting with someone's content will always pour out. So, instead of interacting with new people to grow your follower numbers, focus on engaging with those you already follow. Focus on building relationships with people that you genuinely care about getting to know - because if you're following someone, it should be because you care about what they have to say. And don't force it. Don't sit down with a goal to comment on ten people's content a day. When you feel the need to comment, comment. Otherwise, don't. Or, set aside specific time to engage, but go into it with a few specific people in mind that you'd genuinely like to connect with.

Even though these relationships are virtual, I've found that imagining each one as an in-person relationship can be helpful. When you meet someone new and cultivate a friendship, it takes weeks of occasional texting and getting together a few times to build that relationship. Building a relationship with someone new in an online capacity will take even longer because the interactions are smaller. Let those evolve naturally instead of forcing it.

Bots

Similar to trying to spend your time cold messaging and getting in front of new audiences, you can pay to have bots do the work for you. They troll around on certain hashtags, and when other creators use those hashtags, they'll leave a comment of your choice on those posts.

Instead of spending all that time finding your own people to comment on, the bot does it for you. Instead of only being seen by fifty new people a week, a bot can help get you in front of hundreds, maybe even thousands.

You'll grow your following quickly, which will help with any sponsorships or partnerships you're trying to accomplish, as well as give you instant credibility. What could go wrong?

Well, for one - just like with the previous tactic, anyone who has been around social media and the online business space for more than five minutes can quickly tell that you're using bots. Which is usually an immediate "no." More than likely, you'll end up with tons of new followers that are also bots or are using bots.

For two, in order to give the bot a comment to leave that makes sense - it's going to have to be the most generic of the generic. "I love what you have to say." or "Great post.". Not only does this do absolutely nothing to build relationships, but we all see right through it.

For another thing, if someone does click over to your page, your follower count is going to be a tell-tale sign. A super high number of followers but a super low number of people that you're actually following? Yeah, that only works if you're Taylor Swift. On top of that, if you only have a handful of posts yourself, it's another huge red flag. Because if you aren't Taylor, you did not amass that many followers from a handful of posts.

And the final giveaway - and what's going to harm you in brand partnerships is your engagement rate. Have over 10,000 followers and only 15 likes on your last post? That's a 0.15% engagement rate. Brands aren't going to hand over money for that. They want to leverage your engaged audience, not just a big one.

The bottom line - don't use bots and try to cheat the system.

Trends

Unless you're a content creator for content creation's sake (which, you probably haven't read this much of a book geared towards business owners if you are), trends are best used sparingly. And yet, we can often get wrapped up in feeling like we need to create trending content to be seen and gain new followers.

When it comes to trends, yes, they have the potential to help you see "viral" growth. Getting in front of thousands or even millions of new audience members sounds incredible, in theory. But if your content isn't aligned with your messaging, those new audience members won't bring in sales, which is what we are looking for from our audience members. And if all you're creating is trend-based, your originality completely disappears - leaving you right back to speaking to everyone and no one.

Not to mention that, once again, trying to keep up with trends is time-consuming. (*Is it clear yet that I believe simplicity has a lot to do with using your time wisely?*) If the majority of your content is based on trends, that means you have to spend a lot of time on the app to know what those trends are. And then, when something is trending, you have to act fast and create your own version. And then you're right back to how time-consuming posting in real-time is. Only this time, you're posting AND creating in real-time.

But I don't think trends are all bad and that you should never use them.

Instead, I like to think of my content as a sundae. For the most part, I create educational content around my area of expertise - in my case, simplicity-focused content marketing and launch strategy. These foundational pieces of content are the base of the sundae - the ice cream. It's the part you crave, and it makes or breaks whether you enjoy your sundae. *The toppings will never save a sundae full of banana-flavored ice cream.*

Sundae Formula

Trending Content

"Me" Content

Foundational
Pieces of Content

Then, you've got your hot fudge, or your marshmallow topping, or your caramel. Whatever your "drippy" topping of choice is. This is where I like to bring in my own little personality and quirks with some content around the things that make me - me and that brings out the "personal" in my personal brand. As a reminder, there are five things that my audience knows about me. 1) I'm obsessed with my cats. 2) There's no one I'd rather spend time with than my husband. 3) I love Disney. 4) I read a lot. 5) I spend entirely too much time invested in University of South Carolina sports.

It might seem silly to ever include these types of topics in my content, but these are connection points. Other book lovers know I'm always interested in a book recommendation, and vice versa. Other Disney lovers are always down for a discussion on the latest news. Other college sports fans get the intensity that is the South Eastern Conference. They have nothing to do with "business", but they build relationships with the people that follow you, and with the people you follow if you find they have similar interests.

And finally, the sprinkles on top. *This* is where trending content comes in. The educational content, and the relationship-building content are so important for building and nurturing relationships with the audience you already have. And when you can sprinkle in a trend here and there, the strategy is to bring in new people that will continue to be nurtured through your other content.

The other beauty of sparingly using trending content is that you 1) save time but 2) can be picky about what trends you're doing. If you're focusing on creating trending content, it can feel like you need to participate in every single trend. Which quickly turns into chaos and overwhelm from trying to keep up. But if you're only posting the occasional trend? You can wait until the right trend finds you, and you actually feel *inspired* rather than forced.

And then, when you do bring in new followers from trending content, they can come back to your profile and see all of the other foundational content you've created to decide whether or not to give you a follow. Thus, bringing in and nurturing the *right* audience. (Which leads to more sales down the road.)

The bottom line is that when you're focusing on the four practices above, or any others in a similar vein that are the "next best hack" for growing your followers, your focus isn't in the right place. Sure, growth is great. The bigger the audience, the more sales, yes. But that's *only* true if your audience is filled with the right people. And finding the right people takes a lot more intentionality than just trying hacks for growth. It takes building relationships.

Now that we've talked at length about what *not* to focus on to see growth, it's time to discuss growth strategies that you can use to successfully grow your audience.

Action Step:

If you're doing any of these practices (worrying about the algorithm, cold messaging, bots, focusing on trends) - stop.

Additional Resources:

Chasing Simple Episode 071: The Worst Advice I've Heard about Content Marketing
https://amandawarfield.com/071-2/

For full resources in one place, head to:
https://amandawarfield.com/chasing-simple-marketing-bonuses/

FIVE
LEVERAGE GROWTH STRATEGIES

I was sitting on the floor with my laptop in my lap and my microphone between my legs. I had eight pages of notes to my right, just outside the closet, and all my clothes hanging above me. The *entire* time the podcast host was interviewing me, my body was vibrating with the shakes, and even after the interview, I had to go for a walk to burn off some of the adrenaline coursing through my body.

This was the day that I discovered the magic of podcasting for my business.

It was also the day that I discovered the magic of utilizing content marketing in conjunction with other types of marketing - and the importance of relationships with other business owners.

Until I started connecting with other business owners, I had spent the last eight months working with my head down. In my mind, I was breaking away from working for someone else, and that meant going solo and doing things on my own. I'd been working in a bubble. Doing things entirely by myself, hoping and praying that others would notice, and being frustrated when they didn't. Wondering things like:

How does this person get so many shares of their content? I see them re-sharing the shares, but what is so special about their content that they're getting those shares in the first place? What is mine missing?

How does that person get so many comments on their content? What makes someone decide to comment? I'm using calls to action, and nobody is taking action.

All these questions bounced around in my mind, and the only answer I could think of was that *I* was the problem. That my content wasn't good enough. That I couldn't help anyone. If I could do better, be better, I'd start getting shares of my content and comments and people finally taking action on those calls to action.

It took me finally stepping outside my comfort zone and connecting with another creator/business owner for it to click. It all came back to relationships. Shocking, I know.

By taking that step toward someone else and building a relationship with them, I realized I had someone else's content that I was invested in. I was excited to see their content come across my feed. I was excited to tune into their podcast. And I naturally had things to say and comment on. It stood to reason that that would also be the same for them.

Which leads me to what is the most critical piece of advice for growing your business - don't market (or do business) alone.

Building relationships with other business owners is extremely important. Those friendships will be vital for you on the more challenging days, and it will be nearly impossible to see growth in your business without relationships with others that will help you along the way. Once you've built relationships, you can leverage those to implement various growth strategies. These strategies are vital for getting in front of new people and bringing them into your audience so that you can nurture them.

There are two types of growth strategies: organic and paid. Organic growth strategies utilize avenues that are free and paid strategies, well, you pay for. Within each of those, there are a multitude of different methods you could implement to help grow your audience.

As you read this chapter, remember that not every strategy is essential to implement right now. In fact, most of these won't be something you'll be ready to start implementing until you're a few years into your business journey. We'll discuss how to know when you're ready for each of these in Chapters Seven, Eight, and Nine of the book when we discuss the three phases of a business journey. Take them in for now, but don't start planning to implement anything just yet.

Organic Growth Strategies

Collaborations

When it comes to collaborations with other business owners, the possibilities are only as endless as your imagination. Guest podcasts or blog posts, guest workshops in each other's communities, summits, bundles, and more. As discussed in the previous chapters, different collaborations lend themselves more naturally to different phases of business and their objectives. Objectives you may have as you head into collaborations:

- Improve your Credibility
- Grow your Email List/Audience
- Make Sales

In all honesty, each collaboration you do will likely touch on more than one of the above objectives. However, not all collaborations are made equal. Some will require much more time and effort than others, so I've broken the examples into two categories.

Less Time-Consuming Collaboration Examples:

- Writing a Guest Blog Post for Someone Else's Website
- Being a Podcast or Youtube Guest
- Hoping on a Live for a Social Media Platform

More Time-Consuming Collaboration Examples:

- Speaking Engagements (In-Person and Virtually)
- Joint Venture Webinars: You create a live presentation intended to sell your offer and present it to someone else's audience, and they get a cut of the revenue made from the said presentation.
- Bundle Contributions: A popular growth strategy as I'm writing this book, a group of business owners team up and contribute a digital offer (course, template, etc.) to be bundled together with all of the other contributors' offers and then offered at an extreme discount to everyone's audience.

These examples are certainly not exhaustive, as there are so many ways to connect and grow your network *while* giving back to each other as collaborators.

That's the thing about collaborations - both parties give, and both parties "take." Someone is giving their time and experience in exchange for getting in front of a new audience. The other is providing access to their audience in exchange for unique and valuable information being given to the said audience. This encourages the audience to return for helpful information from both parties.

When you're inviting experts outside of your area of expertise to teach your audience, you're giving your audience great value, which boosts your own content. When you show up as the expert for someone else's content, you're pouring into their audience and potentially growing your own audience. So, collaborations boost your business and content in and of itself, but it also boosts your content and theirs by the nature of having relationships.

Now that you have a relationship with that business owner, you're going to be much more likely to interact with their content now that you have a relationship, and vice versa. This boosts your engagement rate, which boosts who the algorithm pushes your content out to. And while we aren't going to spend any extra time worrying about the algorithm, pleasing it is always a nice side effect of building relationships. So, how do you begin to collaborate with others?

Leverage Your Content for Collaborations

The simplest and least terrifying way to begin collaborating is to invite other experts you admire into your own content. If you're a blogger, ask someone you'd like to have a relationship with to submit a guest post. If you're a podcaster, invite someone you admire to be interviewed on your show. If you're a YouTube creator, do a video interview. Invite them to be part of a live on your social media or as a guest in your email newsletter. The possibilities are endless - consider what you're already creating and how you can invite someone else in.

I often see podcast hosts that only put out solo episodes frustrated by a lack of rapid growth. The problem is that they aren't inviting others into their world. Your content can be the best there is, and your audience members can love it, but the truth is that they don't have a significant incentive to share about it. Some will, absolutely. But if you invite someone else into your world as a guest? They're going to share about it because it benefits them as well. It showcases that someone else believes they're an expert and that they know what they're talking about. Their audience will also hear about that guest episode, opening the doors to new audience members. You'll see more growth, more quickly, if you're inviting others in and they're also sharing your content with their audience.

Pitch Yourself for Collaborations

The second way? Pitch yourself to be part of someone else's content. This is scary, but it's a great way to reach new audiences. As someone who has been creating content for years, it does get exhausting always coming up with new ideas. You might get ignored, or you might get told no. In fact, you'll likely get more nos than yeses. But each time you put yourself out there, someone else learns about your name and business. Each time you put yourself out there, there's a chance they'll say yes.

How do you go about pitching yourself? Here's a quick rundown:

STEP ONE: Determine what you can share to help your ideal audience. Come up with your topic, your end goal, and your main points to get them to that goal. Even better? Come up with three to five questions you can give the host to ask you if you'll be pitching for a podcast or YouTube channel.

STEP TWO: Do your research and create a list of blogs, podcasts, or YouTube channels you'd like to pitch yourself to. Make sure that everyone you put on your list will have your same audience or an adjacent audience that can benefit from your area of expertise. (An adjacent audience is a group of people that aren't your target audience but are close to them. For example, if you sold diapers, parents would be your target audience, but grandparents would be an adjacent audience.) You'll also want to make sure they are accepting guest pitches and that they utilize guests. If they don't, they won't be worth taking the time to pitch to.

STEP THREE: Draft your pitch, and turn it into an email template you can reuse repeatedly. Do yourself a favor and when you're pitching yourself for someone else's content, don't tell them about yourself and how great you are - tell them how you can help their audience. Because you have no relationship with this business owner yet, they don't care about you. They care about giving their audience valuable content. That's where you need to focus your pitch.

If you'd like a sample pitch email template, you can download one at https://amandawarfield.com/pitch-email/

STEP FOUR: Refine your pitch list. Choose which opportunities you'd like to pitch to from your earlier list first. Then, it's time to do your final research. The more you know about their platform, the better your pitch will be.

STEP FIVE: Take what you know about their platform and use that information to update your email template for this specific opportunity. That way, each pitch you send out is uniquely crafted for each opportunity.

STEP SIX: Hit send. And don't forget to follow up. I usually wait one to two weeks before sending a quick follow-up email, but you will most definitely want to follow up. The vast majority of my accepted pitches come from the follow-up, not the initial email.

The bottom line? Don't be afraid to ask. The worst they can say is no. And if you get a no, what have you lost? Not much. But if you get a yes? You could gain a new friend or business contact and be part of creating an even better piece of content.

Word of Mouth Referrals

Word of mouth referrals are a growth strategy that's especially important to lean into in the early years of business. Clients that love the work you do for them will naturally share about your business when opportunities arise - referring you to others by word of mouth.

Referrals from business friends are just as likely as referrals from a previous client. When you've made connections with someone and helped them out in some way, you've showcased yourself as the expert in your area of expertise. When someone else they know needs someone with your type of expertise? You will be the first person they think of and likely recommend.

And why does that matter? Recent studies have shown that word of mouth marketing is the most valuable type of marketing there is, with over 92% of consumers believing the recommendations of friends and family over advertising[5]. If you look at your own life, you'll probably see that play out repeatedly. You might see an ad for something and not think anything else about it again until someone tells you how incredible and must-have it is. And then all of a sudden, you're much more interested in looking into it further.

I watched this play out in my own life recently. Russell and I have been throwing around the idea of getting a self-scooping litter box for the cats for years. But once we started researching, we always ended up too overwhelmed and never made any moves. Frankly, we've had enough potential litter box issues to last a lifetime, and it feels easier to keep scooping it myself.

However, a few months ago, Russell was playing video games with a friend who had recently gotten an automatic scooping litter box. This friend was telling Russell all about how incredible it was, how their cat wasn't having any issues with it, and how nice it was not to have to scoop it themselves anymore. Russell was all in. He had his friend send him the link, and he sent it to me, ready to buy it.

The price? Eight HUNDRED dollars. And Russell was ready to buy it simply because his friend had given it such a glowing review. I, however, did not get the review and immediately hard passed on that purchase without a second thought. Word of mouth truly makes all the difference.

The best way to take advantage of word of mouth marketing? Give, give, give. Pour into your business relationships. Cheer the people in your corner on. Keep their name in your mouth. When someone needs an expert, shout their name from the rooftops. It may seem counterintuitive, but the more you cheer on and boost up others, the more they will do the same for you.

What does word of mouth marketing have to do with your content? Well, once someone refers someone else to you, they will do what we all do and stalk your social media, where they'll find all of your incredible content confirming precisely what their friend said - that you're the expert in your field.

Networking

You might be wondering, isn't networking the same as collaborating and word of mouth marketing? While they all go hand-in-hand, networking is different enough that I wanted to ensure I put a separate section in this chapter about it.

Collaborations tend to be one-on-one activities, where you're inviting one other business owner in and getting to know them on a certain level. Of course, there are group collaboration activities like summits, conferences, or bundles, but even with those, you're inviting those other entrepreneurs in personally one at a time.

On the other hand, networking is like drinking through a fire hose. Instead of one-on-one connections, you're walking into a larger group of other business owners and trying to make connections based on what you have in common, usually in a short amount of time. It would help if you were thinking of how you can connect each new person you meet with someone already in your circle.

Admittedly, networking is not my favorite way to build relationships with other business owners. I always meet incredible people, but I'm an introvert to my very core, and meeting many people at once can be overwhelming. However, it's also really beneficial, and I still push myself to attend networking events each month.

If you're an introvert like me, or networking feels overwhelming for another reason, here are a few things that have helped me:

1. Finding a networking group that's niched down. Instead of just going to a general chamber of commerce event (not that there's anything wrong with those - they can feel more daunting, particularly to introverts), I found a chapter of The Rising Tide Society in my area. From my research, I knew I was walking into a group of local small business owners who valued making connections and lifting each other up. Knowing that I had things in common with others in the group made it easier to connect once I'm there.

2. Have a couple of questions ready. A simple go-to is to ask about someone's business, but if you can think of one or two

more to keep in your back pocket, it will make continuing a conversation much easier.

Here are a few you can use:

What do you do, and how did you get started doing that?
What is your most used (or favorite) business tool right now?
What big goal or project are you currently working on?

I also like to have a few related to my own business ready. For example, asking if they've found any marketing strategies particularly helpful for their business. This is a great way to hear more about how other business owners think about marketing, and it also opens the door for them to ask questions that will help me showcase my expertise as a marketing strategist.

3. Set a goal for yourself. Each month when I walk into a networking event, my goal is to connect with one new person. After going a handful of times and connecting with others, I quickly found "my people." And as an introvert, I would love to stand in the corner and talk to "my people" for the entire event. But I know that to use my time wisely, I'm there to make new connections. Thus, my one person rule. Once I've made one new connection, I'm free to be a wallflower.

How do you make the most of those networking relationships you're building? By being genuinely interested in those people and building strategic partnerships. If you meet someone you know your audience could learn from, hop on a call with them and ask about their business and audience. Who are their ideal clients? Is there anyone you have in mind who could be a good fit for what they offer? If so, introduce them. Send them a message and explain why they should know each other. Ask them into your space - whether by hosting a workshop together or by being a guest expert for your content. Outside of the change from one-on-one collaborations to being around groups of people, networking works very similarly to collaborations in regard to your content marketing. Take an interest in what they're doing, and serve them well. It all leads to more word of mouth referrals.

Search Engine Optimization

Search Engine Optimization (SEO) is the process of trying to be ranked highly on a list of results by a search engine. We typically think of Google, Bing, or Yahoo! when we think of search engines. But Pinterest, YouTube, and even some social media platforms now are also search engines or using search engine technology. When you optimize your content for search engines, you're more likely to bring in new traffic from outside of your "circle" to your website.

SEO is a long game - it can (and often does) take years to start seeing results from optimizing your content, but it's always worth doing as you create your content. A lot goes into strong SEO; I'm not an expert on this and will not pretend to be. But one thing to start doing now is to ensure that every piece of content you create begins with a keyword in mind.

More specifically, you want to have a long-tail keyword in mind. These phrases have five to eight words and are directly related to the topic you're talking about. An example would be "best running shoes for marathon training." These long-tail keywords tend to be less searched for and thus have less traffic, but because they're so specific, they tend to convert better than using just one or two keywords. The goal should be to rank highly for as many long-tail keywords (using your long-form content) as possible so that you're bringing in a trickle of leads from many key phrases. That trickle from multiple pieces of content forms together to create a larger flow of more specified leads.

The opposite would be a short-tail keyword, which are typically one to three words. For example, these would be something like "running shoes," "marathon shoes," or "long-distance shoes." They generally have higher search volumes and higher traffic and can bring in more traffic than a long-tail keyword would. It's harder to rank for some of these, so instead of a trickle from many pieces of content, you'd more likely end up with a flow from a few pieces of content.

Long-Tail Keyword   Short-Tail Keyword

Short-Tail Keywords Bringing in Traffic Together

I enjoy using mostly long-tail keywords and sprinkling in some short-tail keywords now and then, but you can play around with both to see how they work and bring in traffic.

You don't need to be an expert in SEO to get started applying keywords to your content, but how do you choose which keywords to use? First, think about the topic of your piece of content and also what your end goal is for that piece of content. Then, try to step into the shoes of your ideal audience member. What words or phrases are they thinking about in relation to your main topic? Then, type the keywords or phrases you've come up with into Google's search bar. It will auto-populate suggested searches that may give you additional ideas for other key phrases.

Once you know your keyword or phrase, you create your piece of content with that in mind. Find the SEO guidelines for your platform of choice (not listed here so as not to give you outdated advice) and use those to optimize your content for search engines. Then, be patient and allow your SEO ranking to build over time.

By using keywords in your long-form content, as you start to rank for various keywords, you'll begin showing up in these Search Engine results. The more your content is shown to people, the more traffic you'll get to your website - meaning you'll want to have some email capture (like a freebie) for people to sign up for so that you can get them onto your email list.

Not only is SEO great for your long-form content, but some social media platforms are also beginning to utilize search engine optimization. So, keep keywords and phrases in mind as you create your content.

Public Relations

Public Relations, or PR, is not just for the rich and famous. We're likely most familiar with this term regarding that, though - some public figure or corporation makes a misstep in the public eye, and they bring in their PR agency to smooth things over and distract the public with content about something else. Or, there's a big piece of news they need to release (like a divorce or break up) about themselves, and their publicist gives the information they want to be released to a news and media outlet. However, that's not the only way PR works.

PR is building relationships with media, journalists, and other content avenues to gain exposure. In the online business sphere, many entrepreneurs will either hire PR teams or do it themselves to focus on getting appearances in front of other people's audiences. This includes everything from guesting on a podcast to writing a guest article for a magazine like Forbes to trying to land in the news.

When you leverage PR and get in front of new audiences, you can bring them back into your own content sphere and have plenty of content for them to enjoy to get to know you and your brand better. Your content does the work for you.

Affiliate Marketing

Affiliate marketing is a spin-off of word of mouth referrals, with the incentive of getting paid for sharing about someone's product. This method is very common with business owners who are selling an offer or product on a mass level (physical products, courses, digital downloads, etc.); it's a great way for purchasers who would naturally share about an offer anyway to also make some money from sharing. The customer shares about a product they loved and found helpful; they share a link specific to themselves, and then when someone purchases through that link, a percentage of the sale is awarded to the affiliate.

Technically, this method could also fall under the paid marketing category, but because it's something you won't pay for until and unless the sales happen and because it's heavily relationship-based, I decided to include it in the organic marketing category.

With affiliate marketing, you can leverage the relationships of the consumers you already have to reach a wider audience by giving out commissions for sales made through affiliates. The beauty of this type of marketing is that you have legitimate customers who love what you created enough to share it with their audiences, and they can make money promoting your offers, but you don't need an upfront budget for it because the affiliate is only paid for the sales they make.

As I mentioned previously, this is more of an advanced strategy because creating an affiliate program is a lot of work. You have to provide your affiliates with all of the marketing materials they would need, and you must deeply know your messaging for your specific offer so that the materials work well. If they aren't getting sales from sharing about your product, they won't continue sharing about it. On top of that, you have to have your offer concretely created, and you've got to keep your affiliates up to date on what's happening within your offer and the affiliate program. A lot of management goes into this, so I'd recommend waiting until you're in an established place along your business journey to utilize this growth strategy.

Paid Growth Strategies

These final three ways to utilize your content marketing in conjunction with another method are, admittedly, not relationship-based. Each of these will require a marketing budget and are certainly best reserved for when you've established enough to risk that money.

Influencer Marketing

Influencer marketing is a way to promote your products through endorsements from influencers and other content creators online. If an influencer's audience aligns with your audience, and your brand values align with the influencers, they might be a good fit for a campaign for one of your offers.

You'll need to decide the campaign's goal and the type of content you're looking for, but your marketing money will be best spent if you give the influencer you're working with creative freedom. If their content feels off-brand to their audience, they're much less likely to take that next step and check it out. Elyse Meyers is an excellent example of someone who can create incredible, on-brand ads. They don't feel any different from her typical content. Giving an influencer creative freedom is essential, which is why understanding your exact goals for a campaign is crucial before you ever approach an influencer for this type of collaboration.

Sponsor Marketing

Another way to leverage someone else's audience is to sponsor an event they're putting on. Your sponsorship helps them fund their event, and in return, they help promote your business during the said event. When you know that their events' audience aligns closely with your typical customer, it's a partnership worth exploring. What sponsors receive for their sponsorship varies widely by event and event host, so be sure to communicate about that. Some examples include additional content created about your brand, being mentioned and featured at the event, and so much more.

Paid Ads

Ads are everywhere. From Google ads to television ads to advertisements on the games we play on our phones, they surround us. We're so inundated with them to the point that we almost don't even notice them anymore. Yet many entrepreneurs have found success using ads to "pay to play."

Essentially, the idea is that you create some great content that converts, and then you throw money behind it to get it in front of more people. Since you already know that it converts and what the conversion rates are, you know how much you need to spend to bring in a certain amount of new leads each month.

I have clients that use ads to grow their podcast downloads or YouTube subscribers. I have clients that use ads for free downloads to get a swarm of warm leads onto their email list. I also have clients that use ads for low-ticket products that make it easy for the right audience members to say yes. This gets them on their list and helps pay for the cost of the ads. Those who find a conversion rate that allows them to break even on their ads can bring in tons of new leads each month - without spending an arm and a leg on marketing. Then, they can use their sales funnel to sell higher-priced items to those leads to increase their revenue.

However, in recent years, privacy concerns over data (which is how ads know who to target) have been growing, and rightfully so. This recent shift has put a significant dent in the returns in the ad-space land, making it almost impossible to see consistent results with your ads. Does this make ads obsolete? No, but you must budget for them and not expect them to be your only growth strategy.

Do I think there will be some new way to "pay to play" in the future? Absolutely. We're a capitalistic society, and people are constantly finding new ways to make money. But this recent shift has highlighted the importance of relationships within your business. It's great if you can pay to play, but there's a reason we see cycles of revenue-generating activities. Someone figures out a great way to make money, and many people start doing it. Concerns pop up, and suddenly it's not such a great way anymore. Through it all - relationships are always a sure bet.

Just like in *The Princess and the Frog*, when Tiana and Prince Naveen team up to defeat Dr. Facilier, two are almost always better than one. Connecting with other business owners is an incredible way to boost your content marketing instead of letting it drift alone by itself.

As we go into this next chapter, keep in mind that growth for the sake of growth isn't going to take your business where you want to see it go in the long run. Instead, we want to make sure we're intentionally planning for growth in your bottom line - which is the most critical metric for the health of your business. To do so, we need to understand the two parts of a marketing strategy.

Action Step:

Choose one growth strategy to begin applying alongside your content marketing.

Additional Resources:

Chasing Simple Episode 102: Want to See Growth? Here's Your Next Step.
https://amandawarfield.com/102-2/

Sample Pitch Email
https://amandawarfield.com/pitch-email/

For full resources in one place, head to:
https://amandawarfield.com/chasing-simple-marketing-bonuses/

SIX
EDUCATE. ENTERTAIN. CONNECT. SELL

I was going through a marketing course I'd bought, with my calendar printed out in front of me and my rainbow of pens lying beside my computer so that I could color-code my plan by platform.

I felt so proud of myself for making an investment in my business, and I was on top of the world. I was finally going to get my marketing together. Up until that point, I'd spent hundreds of hours researching and trying to mimic what other entrepreneurs were doing in their content. While reviewing "content plans" on Pinterest, the plans that came up were full of "International Donut Day" and "Wacky Sock Wednesday" - absolutely none of which helped me to grow my audience, build relationships, or make sales. I was ready to finally figure out this marketing thing and decided investing in a course from an expert was going to solve all of my problems.

Only, as I sat there and watched the course, I felt confused. The instructor gave all kinds of information, but it felt like there were giant holes in the information presented.

I was told I was supposed to use a theme for each month of content, but HOW? What was I supposed to do to determine said theme? And what was the purpose of theming the month? How did that help?

I'd spent all this money and still felt like I had no idea what I was doing. I internalized that, clearly, I wasn't meant to be good at marketing because I didn't get it.

Friend, if you've had these thoughts, please know I'm wrapping you up in a virtual hug. Because they just aren't true.

The problem isn't you. It's a lack of foundational teaching on where to begin, what a strategy should look like, and the WHY behind your marketing.

Strategy vs. Plan

All too often in the online business space, the terms content strategy and content plan are used interchangeably. But they aren't the same, and unfortunately, we believe that our content plan is our strategy. Hence the disconnect I was feeling with this marketing course I took. I thought I was getting an education on strategy, but all I was learning about was creating a plan.

STRATEGY VS PLAN

CONTENT STRATEGY	CONTENT PLAN
An overarching guide to what you're going to create based on data and goals.	A map of what you're going to talk about and when.

A content plan simply outlines what you will talk about and when. It's when you pull up your digital calendar, or if you're old-school like me, you print out a blank calendar and start using that pen rainbow to mark what's being posted throughout the month.

You assign each platform a color and decide how often you'll post to each platform. You take that platform's color and start marking every time you'll post to the platform by writing its name on each assigned square.

Then, you go back in and assign random topics to each piece of content throughout the month by pulling them out of thin air or rotating from a list you plopped together.

That's a content plan.

It showcases when and where you're posting and what you're talking about when you post.

A content strategy, on the other hand, is your overarching guide to what you're going to create based on data and goals. You have to have an end in mind before you can create your strategy, and you need to understand where you currently sit with your business and your marketing.

For example, maybe you have an offer or product that you want to sell. You'll want to have that in mind as you create your content strategy and then content plan. To use that information to create your content strategy, you'll need to understand the action you want your audience to take (purchasing your offer), and you'll need to understand your messaging in order to guide your audience through the customer journey they'll need to undergo to be ready to purchase. Chapter Nine will discuss the customer journey in detail, but can you see how there's more to deciding what to post than just rotating through a list of topics?

You can think of your content strategy as a building's support and inner structure, while you think of the plan as the design elements of the building. Without the strategy, the content you put out isn't likely going to stand up for your business.

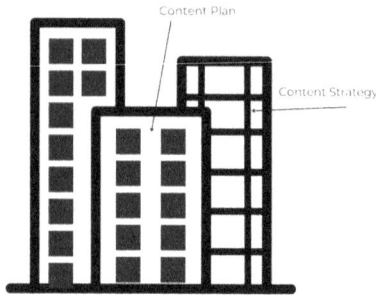

A strategy is the blueprint, and a plan is how you execute said strategy. But, all too often, we start with the plan and skip the strategy. So what we're executing doesn't mean a whole lot to our businesses and doesn't increase our sales and revenue.

It's important to note that there should always be two parts to your marketing strategy:

- Nurture Strategy
- Growth Strategy

In Chapter One, you were introduced to my client, Elsie, who was consistently putting out content to nurture her audience, but she wasn't doing any work to get in front of new audiences. Because she only had a nurture strategy, she wasn't seeing growth in her audience size. Both are necessary for a fully functioning marketing strategy.

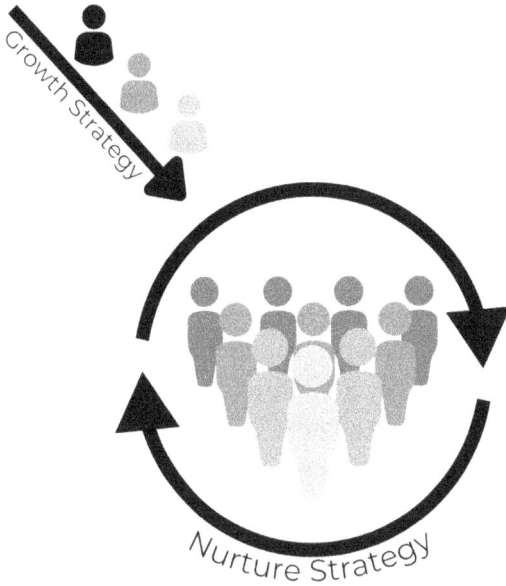

Nurture Strategy

We'll start with the nurture strategy, as this is where content marketing comes into play. With this strategy, the focus is to spend time nurturing your current audience, which means showing up for them consistently, giving value and education, and leading them into your sales processes (because, remember - sales and marketing aren't the same things).

When you're creating and publishing content, you're building relationships with your audience members. We've discussed the importance of building the Know, Like, and Trust factor; building those relationships through your content is critical to every marketing strategy. Particularly, to your nurture strategy within your marketing strategy.

Within your nurture strategy, you'll also want to keep in mind that every piece of content you create should have a few things:

1. A purpose. The main four are educating, entertaining, building relationships (connecting), and selling. Any given piece of content will likely have more than one or all four purposes. But if it's not doing any of the above? It's probably not worth creating for your business.

2. Strong Hook. Our attention spans are short - you've got to learn to grab your audience's attention right from the beginning by making them want more. For example, this book's very first sentence? "I started batching my content because a dog had peed on our carpets." That's a hook. Right from the beginning, it made you go, "Huh?" and want to keep reading.

3. Call to Action (CTA). Every piece of content needs to be created with a specific goal in mind. The key is choosing your call to action before you begin writing your content. That way, you ensure you're writing content that will lead toward that goal.

To determine what each of those critical pieces of your content strategy should be, you'll need to know your goals and purpose for each piece of content you put out. How do you know what that is? This will vary depending on where you are in your business journey and your current business goals.

At first, it may simply be to educate, get your ideas out there, and build relationships. Then, as you become more concrete in your business and have offers to sell, it'll be to sell that offer. Later, you'll be focused on scaling and getting people into your email funnels.

If this seems overwhelming or unclear right now, don't worry. We'll cover this in-depth in Chapters Seven, Eight, and Nine. Not to mention that as you get further into your business, things naturally become more apparent. It doesn't all need to come together from the beginning, and you don't need to have your strategy mapped out entirely for the years to come. Be patient, and take things one step at a time.

Growth Strategy

As we saw with Elsie, content marketing cannot exist in a bubble. It's only one-half of a marketing plan. You must also have a growth strategy that gets you in front of new people and brings them into your audience so that you can nurture them.

And no, content marketing should not be your growth strategy.

Can it grow your audience? Sure. Virality happens, which brings in new faces. Your audience might love and share a piece of your content, which will lead to growth. But that growth is a byproduct, not a strategy. If you cannot guarantee that a piece of content will get you in front of new faces, it's not your growth strategy.

An exception here would be when you're a first adopter of a new platform, as discussed in Chapter One. When you hop on early, your likelihood of seeing virality is much higher due to lack of competition, making being an early adopter a potential growth strategy.

What are some other examples of growth strategies? We covered growth strategies extensively in the last chapter, but as a reminder, some examples would be:

- Pinterest
- Guesting on other Podcasts or YouTube shows

- Guest Teaching in Membership Communities
- Attending Events/Conferences Where Your Ideal Client is Attending
- Participating in Bundles

The common denominator on the vast majority of these? Connecting with others in your industry and using those relationships to get in front of their audiences. Then, the goal is to bring those audiences into your own audience so you can build relationships with them with your nurture strategy.

How do you determine what your strategies should be? Your strategy will look different for each phase of business that you're in.

3 Phases of Business

There are a lot of marketing strategies out there, but they don't all make sense for every phase of business. We want to ensure we focus our time and energy on efforts that will be most effective and worthy of our time so that we can simplify. Therefore, we must look at the three phases of business and determine our strategies based on those phases.

Typically, throughout your business journey, your path will look a little something like this:

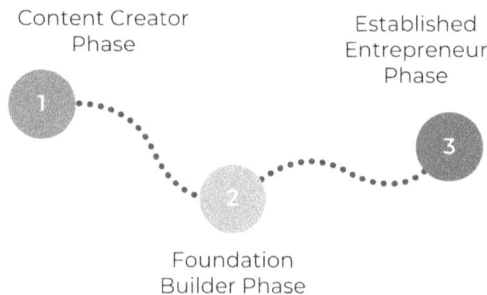

Content Creator Phase

Established Entrepreneur Phase

1

3

2

Foundation Builder Phase

Those three phases are:

Content Creator Phase - Those first few years of owning a business where you're focused on making connections and building relationships. Your nurture strategy is focused on experimenting with your marketing and messaging. Essential growth strategies include networking, referrals/word of mouth, and search engine optimization.

Foundation Builder Phase - In this phase, you know how your business serves others and have at least one offer that sells. Your nurture strategy is about refining your messaging, and your growth strategy is about leveraging the relationships you've been building to get in front of new audiences.

Established Entrepreneur Phase - The later years in owning a business, where you are confident in running your business and really begin to step into your own instead of listening to what all the voices around you tell you that you "should" do. In this phase, you're focusing your nurture strategy on building out and improving your email funnels so that they can sell for you. You're also focused on scaling. This means reaching for more advanced collaborations, working on your public relations, setting up affiliate marketing, and implementing paid growth strategies.

The following three chapters will cover each of these phases in depth. For each phase, we'll go over your overarching business goal, what your nurture and growth marketing strategies should be focused on, and where to focus your messaging within your marketing. That way, you can hone in on where to spend your time and energy instead of being overcome by shiny object syndrome and splitting your attention between many strategies.

Reading these chapters will give you plenty of insight into which phase you're in, but if you'd like to take it a step further, you can take the quiz I've created for you at amandawarfield.com/quiz/ It will tell you which phase you're in, and give you additional resources to dive into alongside the following three chapters to continue to hone your marketing strategies.

Action Step:

Take the "Marketing Strategies to Use Based on Your Phase of Business" Quiz to prepare for reading the next section of the book.

Additional Resources:

Chasing Simple Episode 148: The Part of Your Marketing Plan You Might be Forgetting
https://amandawarfield.com/148-2/

Marketing Strategy Quiz
https://amandawarfield.com/quiz/

Chasing Simple Content Planner
https://amandawarfield.com/planner/

SECTION 2

CLARIFY YOUR BUSINESS JOURNEY

SEVEN

CONTENT CREATOR PHASE

After three years of creating YouTube videos, my client Laurie had thousands of subscribers. She was making money from ad revenue when she decided she wanted to turn this content channel into a full-blown business. Even though she was making some money and she had been creating content and building her audience for years, she was still in what I call the Content Creator phase.

The Content Creator phase is the first of the three phases, and many accidental entrepreneurs begin their journey here. Some people are like Laurie, and they begin their entrepreneurial journey by creating content simply for the sake of creating content. Then, once they build an audience, they realize it's an excellent opportunity for starting a business.

Other people are like me, and they start creating content with the intention of using it to run a business. They may not know exactly how that will work out, but they're confident that they'll be able to figure it out, and the first step is to start creating content.

Both of these types of business owners did not go to school to get a business degree, and they likely didn't grow up wanting to be an entrepreneur. But they saw the possibilities that content creation opened up and jumped in to try it out. They felt the nudge to start a blog, a podcast, or a Youtube channel, and they may have had vague ideas about one day making money from this content but aren't sure what that looks like exactly. In the meantime, they're creating content and building relationships.

If you're spending the majority of your time creating content while still trying to determine what your business will look like or be, you're in the content creator phase as well.

If you're reading this book and thinking, "I skipped this phase completely," that's okay. This phase of business is unique to that accidental entrepreneur. If you dived into running a business knowing exactly what you wanted to do and had a skill to market immediately, this phase wouldn't have played into your business journey. However, I recommend reading this entire chapter, as it has helpful insights into speaking to your audience.

The Content Creator's Business Goal

Now that you know you're in the Content Creator phase of your business journey, what do you do with that information? Remember in Chapter Six we discussed that every piece of marketing needs a purpose. That purpose is going to derive itself directly from your business goals.

In this phase of business, typically, your overarching business goals are to determine how you can use your incredible talents and gifts to help others, what your first offer will be, and making those first sales.

Your biggest struggle is figuring out how to monetize and make money off your content. And you're likely frustrated because you've seen others run their businesses through content marketing, and you know you could too - if you could only "figure it out."

You're spending most of your time on content marketing, and you might feel like you're running in circles, wasting time, and going nowhere fast.

Don't.

With each new piece of content, you're learning something new about content marketing, about what your business may or may not look like, and about yourself as an entrepreneur. At this stage, you're trying to determine your niche (your particular segment or space in your market) and what your place in the business world is going to be. The more you understand your niche, the more you'll understand what your audience needs from you and will be able to create that first offer that sells.

This phase length varies, but it can take years. Especially if you don't have an audience already built up. Personally, I went through three large pivots (with many more minor pivots in between) and about two and a half years before I felt removed from this stage. Give yourself lots of grace and space to not have it all figured out. Your overall marketing strategy based on those business goals is to experiment and have fun. Throw some spaghetti at the wall and see what sticks.

The Content Creator's Growth Strategy

In this phase, your growth marketing strategy is simple - making connections and building relationships. Set aside time to connect with other content creators in your same industry, and ensure you're connecting with other creators/business owners in adjacent industries. For example, if you're focused on creating content around time management for busy moms, a great connection would be someone who helps busy moms create a wardrobe they love. Your topics aren't the same, but your audiences are. In addition, other business owners focusing on time management are great connections, whether their audience is the same or slightly different.

These two types of relationships will be helpful as you further cement your business niche and become ready to start getting in front of new audiences through collaborations. But for now, you'll want to start by making those connections and building relationships.

This can be done virtually and in person, and I highly recommend both. For building relationships virtually, find blogs, podcasts, and YouTube channels you connect with, read/listen/watch the content, and then - here's the key - respond. Leave a comment on the blog post or YouTube video, find the creator on social media and send them a direct message about the content, and share it with your social media audience. And then do it again. Like in-person relationships, a one-time interaction doesn't make you best friends. But over time, your connection points add up.

As for in-person relationship building, find groups in your area created for business owners and groups catered to your audience. A few places to look for events:

- Use social media to search for your town name and keywords about your audience (for example, town name business owners, town name moms, etc.)
- Check out the events your local library is putting on.

- Check to see if there's a Rising Tide Society chapter in your local area.

The Rising Tide Society (co-founded in 2015 by Natalie Franke) is a community of small business owners gathering in the spirit of Community Over Competition ®. There are chapters worldwide, and they are a great way to get plugged in with other creators and business owners in person.

Remember, this strategy can often get pushed to the side as unimportant in those early years of business. It's scary, and you may not feel ready, but I encourage you to start now. Or maybe, it doesn't feel important because you don't see the return immediately. Cultivating relationships takes time, and without relationships in business, you'll find yourself in the same situation as my client Elsie.

The Content Creator's Nurture Strategy

Your nurture strategy during this phase is simple: experiment. Let yourself try out new things. Let yourself have fun. Don't worry so much about having an exact strategy that will take you from zero to six figures this year, and allow yourself to put content out there for the sake of finding where you belong in the online business world.

Here are a few ways you can experiment with your content marketing:

- *Try different platforms and platform features.* Starting out is the best time to experiment with which platforms and platform features you enjoy most.
- *Vary your topics.* We'll discuss this later in this chapter during the messaging section, but talk about different aspects of your expertise you're passionate about to see what sticks with your audience.

- *Change your tone and writing/speaking style.* Eventually, you'll want to stick to one overall brand voice, but for now, play around - experiment with longer content, shorter content, funny content, and serious content. Learn what you enjoy creating and what your audience tends to enjoy most.
- *Switch up your visuals.* If you're creating a lot of video content, try creating graphics or still images.

Please do not be afraid to throw spaghetti at the wall (try out many different ideas and strategies) and see what sticks. In our rush to become "real" business owners in our own eyes, we often try to skip this experimentation step and go straight to trying to piece together some strategy.

However, leaning into this *is* a strategy. It just takes some time and patience. (*Spoiler: so does everything in business*)

A pitfall of this content creation stage is that we don't give ourselves permission to trust our intuition, and we try to copy what other content creators are doing. The problem is that no matter how established your business is, you are *always* experimenting with your marketing. So what you see as the standard is likely a test run of an unknown strategy. Instead of mimicking others, trust your instincts while creating your content.

Marketing Messaging for the Content Creator

You know that your goal during the Content Creator phase is to help you build an audience, make connections, and determine the path forward for your business so that you can create that initial offer. We've discussed the importance of building relationships now, and you've been given permission to experiment with your content.

You might be wondering now, "How do I pull it all together?" and that is where your messaging comes in. While messaging is one thing that you should be experimenting with during this phase, there are three key milestones that you should work towards:

- Understanding Your Audience
- Finding Your Niche
- Doubling Down on What Works

Understanding Your Audience

When you're experimenting with your messaging, you still want to be attracting new people into your audience. The key to doing so is understanding who your audience is - whether that's other business owners or someone in a specific phase of life, such as a new mom or a recent college grad - and being able to speak to them.

No, you don't need to know their favorite color, where they shop, or what magazines they buy. I've found it's far more effective to focus on one overarching theme that bands your ideal audience together (are they moms, business owners, or new college grads, etc.?) and then determine what they're hoping to achieve. If you can get more specific than that, great. But those two things will take you much farther in connecting with them than their favorite vacation spot.

For example, if you hope to help recent grads take the next step in their career, you may not know yet precisely what piece of the puzzle you're filling for them. You may have many talents they would benefit from, including resume creation, job interviewing, offer negotiation, finding the right place to live and put down roots, and so much more. But you haven't decided where exactly you're taking your messaging. So, you're doing as discussed and experimenting with messaging around all of the above.

What you *do* know is that you're speaking to recent graduates. This means that while your content may cover a variety of topics, it's all directed toward those grads.

Knowing who your audience is will give you enough guidance to start throwing ideas out in your content while still seeing growth in your audience. As long as you're talking to the right people, it will be much easier to see what "sticks" for you *and* your audience.

Finding Your Niche

As you're throwing spaghetti at the wall, your goal is to find the topics and messaging you want to move your business into and create that initial offer around, which means finding your niche. Your niche is your specific market segment and is how you differentiate yourself from your competitors. It's what makes your business unique.

Often in the early stages of business, entrepreneurs rebel against the idea that they must choose a niche. It's insulting because they don't have just one passion - they're multi-passionate people, and how dare anyone try to put them in a box?

I certainly felt that way at first. I was a few years into owning my own business before I started to understand why rejecting the idea of a specific niche wasn't in my best interest.

I firmly believe that every entrepreneur out there is multi-passionate. You'd HAVE to be to take on all the tasks necessary to run a business. Who else would want to wear every hat required to keep a business running? If you had only one passion, you probably would have stuck to your previous job and enjoyed being passionate about that one thing.

You've probably heard the phrase, "If you're speaking to everyone, you're speaking to no one." Sounds catchy, but what does it mean?

If you're speaking to everyone, *and* you're all over the place with the things you're passionate about? Well, you aren't going to stand out, which means no one will pay attention to what you're saying. And on top of that, your audience will be confused because your content and messaging will be all over the place.

So, all of those gurus telling you to niche down? They're right. The way to stand out in the online space is by harnessing your passions into one specific expertise.

I'm not saying you need to jump into one particular niche immediately. While you're in this Content Creator phase of starting your business, you should embrace the multiple passions in your heart as long as you realize you're using them to help you eventually niche down.

Need help figuring out how to move forward with narrowing things down? Make a list of all of your passions, and then create a Venn Diagram or two to keep everything top of mind. Try and find those connecting pieces and how you can utilize many of your passions to discover your niche and expertise. Here's what a Venn diagram would have looked like for my business back at the beginning:

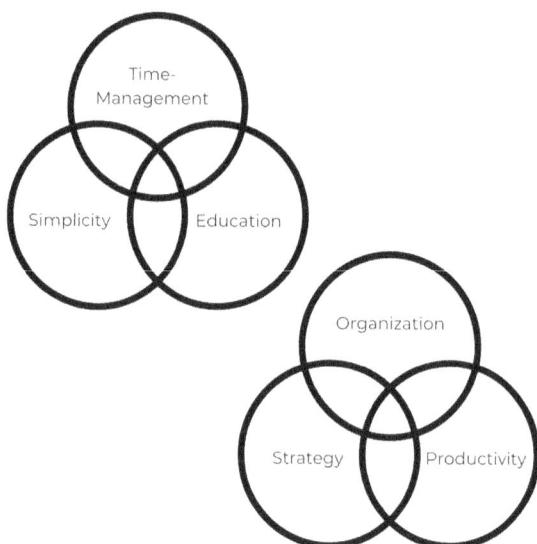

You'll remember me saying earlier in the book that when I felt that call to start a blog, I only knew I wanted to focus on simplicity. But I also wanted to talk about my other passions - time management, productivity, organization and strategy, and education. I just had zero idea HOW to go about doing that. It took a few years and three different iterations of my business, but by trying to find the connection pieces, I finally could nail down the one thing I LOVE doing - simplicity-focused content marketing and launch strategy.

Creating your own Venn Diagram will not be a one-time exercise. In fact, for now, you may only be able to draw the diagram and add the overall passions into it. That's okay and completely normal. Start there, and leave the chart accessible so you can add to it over time. Eventually, your niche will become clear through your experimentation.

Doubling Down on What Works

After spending some time throwing spaghetti at the wall, you will start to see a pattern in what your baseline numbers are around your content. These baseline numbers will be your standard for various interactions within your content. Think about the number of website visitors and viewers per YouTube video or downloads per podcast episode. Of course, the numbers will fluctuate, and you may even see an increase in most months. But, for the most part, your numbers will be in a similar range.

This is the not-so-fun part of using content marketing to grow a business. It's free, but it takes TIME.

As you are going about your weeks and months, take the time to record those baseline numbers. It feels tedious and unnecessary initially, but knowing your baseline numbers is imperative for understanding when a piece of content connects with your audience.

You'll know because you'll have a jump in numbers. Whether that's in views, downloads, comments, or direct messages, there will be an indicator showing you that your audience wants more of that.

Why is this so important? Because you, my sweet content creator friend, are working on creating that initial offer. And when a topic connects with your audience in a way that stands out? That is a huge indicator to experiment with that topic further to look for a pattern. If you see one, you've likely uncovered a pain point and topic for your audience that would be an excellent fit for an offer.

I was in the second iteration of my business, talking to small business owners about time management and productivity when I struck gold. I posted a piece of content that shared how I could create a month's worth of content in just one week, and my notifications blew up.

So, I thought, "Well, that's interesting. I wonder what would happen if I talked about it again?"

And again, I had interactions above and beyond my typical baseline. I was getting significantly more comments and direct messages than ever before.

So, I talked about it again and again. And again and again, my comments and direct messages were higher than usual. Finally, I realized this was it. This is my next step.

From listening to my audience, I created what I consider to be my first foundational offer - Content Batching Bootcamp. This course helps content creators and entrepreneurs create a system for creating a month's worth of content in one week, and hundreds of students have gone through it successfully. It was the offer that truly launched my business into feeling "real."

Did I ever think I would be writing an entire book on content marketing or even have my business solely focus on content marketing?

Absolutely not.

But I knew my next right step was to keep up with that one topic, and I could worry about the rest later.

And that's what I want you to do as well. When something clicks, keep talking about it. If it was a one-time thing, no harm, no foul. But if it wasn't? Like Anna and Elsa in *Frozen*, keep taking the next right step until the vision makes sense for where the journey is taking your business. Before you know it, you'll have your messaging nailed down, your first offer will be making you money, and you'll be moving into the Foundation Builder phase of your business journey.

Action Step:

Find a networking group in your area. (I strongly recommend finding a Rising Tide Society chapter near you.)

Additional Resources:

Chasing Simple Episode 116: Your First Step to Creating a Marketing Strategy
https://amandawarfield.com/116-2/

Content Batching Bootcamp
https://amandawarfield.com/content/

For full resources in one place, head to:
https://amandawarfield.com/chasing-simple-marketing-bonuses/

EIGHT
FOUNDATION BUILDER PHASE

Once Laurie decided to take her content creation and leverage it to build a business, she started with a membership, and that membership community sold well. Over time, she began to wonder, "What's next?". She was seeing growth in her audience and her bottom line, and she knew there was more she could do outside of creating content and running her membership community. This bumped her over to the next phase of the business journey - the Foundation Builder phase.

The Foundation Builder phase is the second of the three phases, and some people start their business here while others spend time in the Content Creator phase first. You've either taken the time to figure out where your place is in the business world, or you knew from the very beginning and had a specific skill and offer in mind from the second you got started. In fact, that skill or offer was likely what made you decide to start the business in the first place.

How do you know if you're in this phase? You can clearly, confidently, and quickly explain who your business serves, how you help them, and what your main offer/service is. You have at least one offer that is selling, and you're starting to see growth and momentum. Meaning that your revenue is growing, your audience is growing, and your connections are growing.

The Foundation Builder's Business Goal

At this stage in your business, your main offer is probably selling well, and your goal is to determine the other foundational offers of your business by creating offers that are complimentary to your main offer. These complimentary offerings will become part of your foundational value ladder. This means having an offer suite that allows your audience to take the next step toward the larger goal of your business.

Remember my course, Content Batching Bootcamp? That was my first foundational offer in my business. After running the course live a few times, I realized that once my students were no longer spending all of their time creating content, they had the mental capacity to think about the strategy of what they were posting, and they were looking for guidance.

1:1 Content
Marketing Strategy →

Content
Batching
Bootcamp →

Thus, the next of my foundational offers was created - a service where I helped clients craft their strategy behind what they were saying in their content. This new offer took my audience up a rung in the value ladder as it was both the next step in working with me on a deeper level and it was the next step in their content marketing needs.

However, I also looked at those in my audience who weren't ready for Content Batching Bootcamp and listened to what they needed. There were many people I talked to that were interested but ultimately didn't enroll because they weren't creating content at all. They knew they wanted to create content, and they thought about it often, but they were so overwhelmed by not knowing *what* to say in their content that they were paralyzed.

So, I created A Year of Content Prompts. This offer gave those audience members exactly what they needed to get started creating their content - something to tell them what to say. In this case, it was the step below Content Batching Bootcamp on the value ladder.

If you're in the Foundation Builder phase of your business journey, you are likely working on creating those foundational pieces of your value ladder for yourself. In order to do so, you must be utilizing your marketing to refine your messaging so that you can convert your audience members into clients or customers and keep your eyes peeled for other ways you can serve them.

The Foundation Builder's Growth Strategy

The growth strategy for this phase is dependent upon whether you went through the Content Creator phase or if you jumped straight into the Foundation Builder phase. If you jump straight into the Foundation Builder phase, you'll combine the Content Creator phase growth strategy with this phase's growth strategy. In the last chapter, I covered that strategy extensively, so you'll want to go back and read it if you skipped ahead. In essence, the focus was all about building connections with others within your industry and starting to form relationships.

In this phase, you'll want to take your growth strategy to the next level by leveraging those relationships that you've been building in order to get in front of your audiences. This helps to get your business name out there and build credibility. Once someone trusts you enough to share about you, their audience sees you as trustworthy. Not only that, but you can turn around and share the fact that others trust you enough to share you with their audiences, which builds even more credibility for your audience members (and future collaborators).

How do you get in front of someone's audience? By helping them create content. As you've likely discovered by this point, coming up with what to talk about in your content can become exhausting. Which is why business owners love to bring in other experts within their content - it's less creation work for them, the guest typically comes with a topic in mind, so the business owner doesn't have to come up with what to talk about, and it offers variety to their audience.

There are many ways and strategies for teaming up with other creators, but starting with joint content efforts is a simple and effective way to begin. Some of the simplest examples are:

- Writing a Guest Blog Post for Someone Else's Website
- Being a Podcast or YouTube Guest
- Hoping on a Live for a Social Media Platform

The simplest way to start is to work with your closest friends to create content for their own platforms. Team up for their content, and then turn around and team up for your content. For example, maybe you hop on a social media live stream on their account, and then the next week, you do the same from your account. Or maybe they have a podcast that you record an interview for, and they come onto your Youtube channel as a guest. Take some time to think about which of this you feel most comfortable with and who you could team up with for something like this.

Once you've gotten your feet wet with guest content, you'll discover which types of content you enjoy guesting on, and you can continue to use those connections you've been creating for further opportunities.

The beauty of this strategy is that you're not only getting in front of new audiences and seeing growth but guesting on other businesses' content creates incredible opportunities for honing your own messaging. When you're being interviewed about the topics you're an expert in, the interviewer will ask you questions that you may never have thought of before. Don't let that scare you - those questions are golden nuggets for you to take back into your own content and nurture strategy, and further flesh out your messaging.

The Foundation Builder's Nurture Strategy

This leads us into what the nurture strategy should be for content in this phase of business. In the last phase, we experimented and threw spaghetti at the wall to see what stuck. Your strategy for the Foundation Builder phase is to continue to refine your messaging. We'll go into the details of exactly how to do that in the next section, but the next three steps for refining your messaging are:

- Narrow Down Your Audience
- Hone in On The Problem You Solve
- Craft Your Content Themes

Often at this phase of owning a business, we can become lazy with our content. If you've been creating for years, you may feel like you've run out of things to say. Or you may be burnt out from so much creation. It becomes rote, where you're slapping down content as quickly as you can. Instead, try to leave space to enjoy diving into the process of going deeper and getting even more intentional with the content you're creating instead of dismissing it as just another item on your to-do list.

Marketing Messaging for the Foundation Builder

Narrow Down Your Audience

When it comes to what to focus on in your messaging at this point in your content marketing strategy, you'll first want to further refine your audience, if you can. If things still feel right from where you refined it during the last phase, you may not need to. But often, as we get further and further into our businesses, we discover new and important pieces of the people we want to speak to.

For example, you may have originally decided that you wanted to speak to business owners that were in the mid-years of their business, and now have decided that you want to speak specifically to small business owners in the photography sphere that are in the mid-years of owning their businesses. See how adding one small detail makes it much easier to picture your ideal audience member?

Take some time to think about whether you've discovered any additional pieces of information about your ideal client. Keeping those details in mind helps ensure your messaging is really pulling in the right people.

Hone in On The Problem You Solve

The next part of your messaging that you want to focus on is the problem you are solving for your clients and your audience. There are a few questions you'll want to be able to answer about that problem:

1. What exactly is the problem that you're solving for your audience/clients?
2. How does said problem affect their life/business?
3. How do you solve that problem for them?
4. What is the outcome of solving that problem for your audience/clients?

Being able to answer those questions will give you more insight into how to showcase your expertise and your offer, as well as give you plenty of ledges to speak to your client from. If you'd like some additional help with this, I created a worksheet for you. You can grab it at https://amandawarfield.com/messaging-worksheet/

Craft Your Content Themes

Ah, buckets. Also sometimes called "pillars". One of the most talked about but least explained pieces of advice when it comes to content marketing.

Often we're told to use buckets as topics to rotate through in our content marketing. We're told to choose five topics and talk about topic "A" in one piece of content, then topic "B" in the next, topic "C" in the one after that ... so on and so forth until you wind back up at "A." Typically, those five buckets are five different passions.

Let's say you're a family photographer. Here's an example of what your buckets might look like:

A - Motherhood
B - Reading
C - Photography
D - Client Reviews
E - Editing

The idea is that by rotating through these different buckets, you're building a personal brand where your audience gets to know and connect with you while also showcasing your business expertise.

The problem with this is that your business content gets lost in the shuffle, and there's no real strategy behind it. You choose five things, and you talk about each of them on a rotational basis, but your content doesn't lead anyone anywhere. There's no journey for your audience to take, and you're not consistently solving their problems.

Plus, if you're talking about five different topics, you're likely confusing your audience as far as what your expertise is because you're all over the map. Using buckets makes more sense in the Content Creator phase, where you're throwing spaghetti at the wall, than it does here, where you're trying to showcase that you're an expert in your field.

However, I understand the appeal of buckets. It's a simple way to make sure you're hitting all of the important parts of your business, and it's an easy way to come up with things to say for your social media. My suggestion is that instead of having five topics you rotate through, you implement five themes:

FIVE THEMES OF SOCIAL MEDIA MARKETING

- Entertainment
- Client/Customer Showcase
- Educational
- Engagement
- Promotional

1. Entertainment - Some people are naturally funny and outgoing, and this type of post is a no-brainer for them. However, entertaining content doesn't have to make someone laugh. It simply has to grab their attention and

make them curious. For example, I love time lapses of just about anything - cleaning, painting, working out. Those types of content are always sure to pause my scrolling because I find them entertaining. These posts are great for letting your audience into your world and expressing who you are so they can get to know you. Your call to action is typically going to be to engage with the content in some way. Within this type of theme, this would be a good place to implement some personal bucket topics.

2. Client/Customer Showcase - in these, you'll want to somehow showcase your expertise and what you do to help others by showcasing your clients/customers in some way. This can be through a testimonial you share, talking about an experience you had with a client/customer, or talking about what it's like to be a client/customer of yours. Your call to action is typically going to be the next steps for how they can work with you.

3. Educational - Here, you want to educate your audience on your area of expertise and how you can solve their problems. These pieces can be just straight informational pieces, or they can lead back to your latest piece of long-form content. These are also a great chance to throw out new ideas you've been thinking of to see how they stick for a potential future offer. Your call to action here will vary but can be anything from asking them to share the piece of content, to commenting on it, to saving it for later, all the way to encouraging them to look at the long-form content that gives more context.

4. Engage - The purpose behind an engaging post is to, well, boost your engagement. They can be as simple as

posing a question to your audience and encouraging their response, or they can be something as complex as stirring up controversy. No matter what direction you take these pieces of content, your call to action is always going to be to have them engage with the content in some way, typically by commenting. However, you can also encourage shares and saves.

5. Promotional - Here's the one most of us avoid, like the plague. The Big Ask. In this kind of post you're selling, you're sharing about a free download you've created, or you're sharing about some sort of collaboration (like a summit or bundle) that you're a part of. Your call to action is going to be along the lines of whatever it is that you're talking about in that post. Examples of calls to action for this type of post would be: to apply to work with you, to buy a digital offer, to sign up for a summit/bundle, or to download your free opt-in.

By rotating through these five themes, you'll make sure to cover a variety of types of content (and do everything from educating to building relationships to selling) without confusing your audience by talking about a wide range of topics. It should be noted that you don't need to blindly rotate through in this exact order over and over again but that you'll want to ensure you're using a mix of all of them throughout the month. Since we all love to avoid these, it's worth the reminder that you probably do need to add more promotional posts into the mix than you plan to, though.

Once you've nailed down the foundational offers in your business, you'll be ready to move into scaling inside the Established Entrepreneur phase.

Action Step:

Download and fill out the worksheet I created for you to dig deeper into the problem you solve and how it helps your audience.
https://amandawarfield.com/messaging-worksheet/

Additional Resources:

Chasing Simple Episode 069: 7 Places to Find Content Inspiration
https://amandawarfield.com/069-2/

Content Batching Bootcamp
https://amandawarfield.com/content/

A Year of Content Prompts
https://amandawarfield.com/a-year-of-content-prompts/

1:1 Content Marketing Strategy
https://amandawarfield.com/ways-to-work-together/

For full resources in one place, head to:
https://amandawarfield.com/chasing-simple-marketing-bonuses/

NINE
ESTABLISHED ENTREPRENEUR PHASE

After nailing down her value ladder, Laurie had three offers - a course, a membership community, and one-on-one coaching. Thanks to the years she spent in the Content Creator phase building an audience, the initial sales and enthusiasm for each offer was high, which boded well for her revenue goals, and her foundational offers that she created in the Foundation Builder phase were selling well.

However, after a few launches, she came to realize there was a problem. Instead of her launches growing, she saw smaller sales. Understandably, she was frustrated because her audience was not small by any means. So why was her bottom line not growing?

Ultimately, the problem was that she was launching to the same people without focusing on growing her audience. Even though her audience in and of itself was quite large, she had not been focusing on growth strategies to continue to bring in new audience members to sell to. Thus, her original launches did well, but with each launch, the audience pool got smaller as more of her audience bought, meaning there were fewer people she was selling to.

If you have been, or are in, a similar place to Laurie, you're likely in the Established Entrepreneur phase. Established Entrepreneurs have multiple offers in their business funnel, and they've got a value ladder that flows from one offer to the next, with each offer up-leveling what an audience member learned/overcame in the previous offer. However, if they aren't intentional about growth, they'll fall into the same trap as Laurie. Selling to the same people over and over and seeing a decline in revenue.

The Established Entrepreneur's Business Goal

Up until this point, you may be in a similar situation to Laurie, where the only time you are selling your offers is when you spend the time and energy hosting a live launch full of events, visibility, and hard selling. In order to sell without having to sell individually and directly to each new student, you will have to set up systems that will sell for you.

You may have heard of the idea of "scaling" in conjunction with growing your business. This means you are working to increase your profitability, usually while decreasing your time spent work-ing. In order to scale your business revenue, you'll need to have those systems set up and then really focus on bringing in new audi-ence members to sell to.

Three main goals to help you do so are:

- Creating email funnels to help sell for you.
- Using data to tweak and improve your funnels for higher conversion rates.
- Focus on scaling to bring in new audience members to your funnels.

Successful scaling, like every phase of business, takes time and patience. As we'll talk about in the data section of this chapter, you'll be making small tweaks and then monitoring the difference each tweak makes. This requires many new people to go through said funnel, so you have to do the work to find new audience members and bring them in. Sometimes the tweak is successful, and sometimes it's not, which means returning to what worked previously or trying something new. The encouraging news is that small changes can make a big difference in your bottom line.

The Established Entrepreneur's Growth Strategy

Because your goal at this stage of business is to see more growth by scaling, you're leaning more heavily than ever into your connections and relationships, and you're doing what you can to get in front of new audiences and then using your marketing to nurture those new faces well.

Teaming up with other business owners and guesting on their content was a great first step in bringing in new audience members. While continuing to leverage those opportunities, it's also time to take things a step further with bigger opportunities, larger audiences, and more selling.

There are many strategies that fall under this category, but here are some examples to consider:

- Speaking Engagements (In-Person and Virtually)
- Joint Venture Webinars. You create a live presentation intended to sell your offer and present it to someone else's audience, and they get a cut of the revenue made from said presentation.
- Bundle Contributions. A popular growth strategy as I'm writing this book, a group of business owners team up and

contribute a digital offer (course, template, etc.) to be bundled together with all of the other contributors' offers and then offered at an extreme discount to everyone's audience.

What makes the focus of these opportunities different from those discussed in the previous chapter is that these are focused on creating a sale in addition to educating. Those in the previous chapter had a larger emphasis on educating and bringing new audience members into your sphere. These still aim to do so, but the larger goal is to do so through selling.

To get started with these bigger opportunities is to pick one that sounds interesting and suited to your skills and confidence level, and then turn to your closest business relationships to test out the process. Once you've gotten more comfortable with the process and discovered what exactly works for your business, you'll be ready to lean on those in your outer circle of relationships and also pitch to those that you have a joint connection with but not a relationship yet. This is also a good time in your business journey to add paid marketing strategies for growth.

The Established Entrepreneur's Nurture Strategy

In this phase of business, you'll be doing more with your nurture strategy than ever before as well. As a reminder, two of your business goals that will focus on your nurture strategy are:

- Creating email funnels to help sell for you.
- Using data to tweak and improve your funnels for higher conversion rates.

Email Funnels

There are three sequences (funnels) you will want to focus on to start: an opt-in sequence, a welcome sequence, and a sales sequence. Each subscriber will be sent through all three before being added to your email newsletter and hearing from you on a consistent basis. For the simplest setup (because these projects certainly won't happen overnight), start with your welcome sequence, then create an opt-in sequence for each free download you have. Finally, add on the sales sequence.

You'll find a full flowchart example in the appendix, but here's a quick breakdown of what that would look like:

- When a new subscriber downloads your freebie, they'll be sent through the opt-in sequence.
- Once they've completed the opt-in sequence, you'll have an automated check (you'll set this up within your email

service provider based on tags) to see if they've already gone through a welcome sequence.

- If not, you'll send them through the welcome sequence.
- If they have, you'll remove them from the opt-in sequence and let them be.
- Then you'll check to see if they've gone through your sales sequence for your signature offer.
- If not, you'll send them through that one.
- And if they have, you'll remove them from the welcome sequence and let them be.

After going through all three, they'll be placed in your newsletter list.

Once you have all three of these funnels set up, your job will be to use your growth strategy opportunities to drive people into the funnel by encouraging them to sign up for the free opt-in you created. This will send them through the entire funnel, with the goal of converting audience members into students/purchasers.

Over time, you'll collect information that will tell you how the funnel is performing and where you can improve for better results. When it comes to data, there are about a million different pieces that you can measure and look at in order to make improvements. The key here is to keep things simple. If you overcomplicate it, you won't do it.

Using Data to Improve Your Content

I track a variety of general numbers. Basic things like which podcast episodes got the most downloads, total downloads, website numbers, which offers sold best during a given month, how many followers I have, etc. Then, on the first of the month, I sit down and fill out my spreadsheet, so I can spot patterns and look for areas to improve. Having these general numbers also allows me to continue experimenting.

If I try something new, I'll most likely see an increase or decrease. Thus, telling me whether or not I should continue with said experimental action. For example, if I decide to try posting less to a certain social media platform, I'm going to want to make sure to keep an eye on my leads and my sales. If they decrease for the next two months, I'll know I should probably go back to posting more (as long as that's not a consistent pattern with sales and leads from the previous year). However, if they stay the same, I'll know I can continue to post less - earning me more time back in my batch week (more on that in Chapter Thirteen).

But at any given time, I'm only paying attention to ONE data set. I track a variety so that I have plenty of data to look back on, but only one set is getting my attention at any given time. And the way I determine that is by looking at my goals.

For example, If there's a particular offer I'd love to see make more sales, I'll start measuring how many eyes actually get on that sales page. I'll brainstorm how to get more eyes on it and increase my efforts. After a month, I'll either see more views or I won't. If I don't, it's back to the drawing board to get more eyes on it.

If I see more views, the next question is - what's the conversion rate (the percentage of people that took action after viewing)? And then, I begin to brainstorm how to increase that rate. Implement one thing, check the data at the end of the next month, and so on and so forth.

Track your numbers, but let your goals determine which ones influence where you try to improve next. Remember that improving your business takes time and a lot of small tweaks. Keep at it, and don't feel the need to fix all of the things at once. Simple is the name of the game.

Using Data to Improve Funnels

When it comes to funnel improvements, you also want to keep things as simple as possible. Choose one funnel and then one small step within that funnel to focus on first. Let's look at how we're using data to help improve Laurie's course sales.

First, we determined our goal and focus. In this case, we wanted to see more sales of her course. In particular, we wanted to focus on her evergreen sales (those coming from her email funnels and not a live launch) and felt that the first step was to improve the course sales page.

Once we knew what our goals were, we had to determine the key performance indicators (KPIs) that we wanted to measure. These indicators give us a baseline to start from, and then we can judge our tweaks against that baseline. If numbers rise, we know a tweak improved our funnel. If they fall, we know they did not. For this project, we chose three KPIs to measure:

- Sales Page Views
- New Students
- Sales Page Conversion Rate

Sales page views indicate how many people land on the sales page and learn more about the course. The number of new students shows us how many sales were made. And the conversion rate from those two numbers (New Students divided by Sales Page Views x

100) tells us what we can expect in sales based on how many people land on that page.

If 200 people land on the sales page, and 30 people purchase the course, that means that the sales page is converting at 15%. (30/200 x 100). From there, we worked to improve the sales page and make changes to see what those changes did to the conversion rate.

You can do this for every step of your funnel, including but not limited to:

- Landing Pages to optimize how many conversions into your funnel you're getting.
- Email Subject Lines to optimize how many of your emails are actually being opened and read.
- Number of Emails to determine how much content someone needs before being ready to purchase.
- Email Copy itself to inform, educate, and sell better.

Now that you're on board with slowly improving your funnels, I know exactly what you're thinking. What conversion rates should you be aiming for?

One percent better than your current average.

It's easy to look up industry averages for conversion rates, but these numbers are often outdated or don't give an accurate picture. Instead, I highly recommend finding your baseline and then competing against yourself to improve whatever that current baseline is.

Marketing Messaging for the Established Entrepreneur

Your messaging focus in this phase of business is to nail down your messaging for your business overall and messaging for each offer that you have because each offer speaks to a different pain point of your audience.

As you are working on creating your value ladder for your business, you'll use what you're learning about your audience to craft your customer journey. There are five phases of a customer journey, and your job is to use your marketing to take your audience from where they are all the way to student/purchaser/client:

- Problem Unaware
- Problem Aware
- Solution Aware
- Offer Aware
- Student/Client

5 Stages of the Customer Journey

Problem Unaware Phase

For your audience members that reside here, they are not even aware of the exact issue that they have in relation to your offer. Your job is to use your content to speak to them where they are in that unawareness so that you can move them into the next phase.

Take Content Batching Bootcamp, for example. An audience member in the problem-unaware phase knows they don't enjoy content marketing, and they likely feel overwhelmed, frustrated, and burnt out by the entire process. What they aren't aware of is that the problem they have is they don't have a system in place for creating content. As far as they know, their problem is they're overwhelmed by content creation.

In order to speak to my audience members in this problem-unaware phase, I have to create content around the problem they *are* aware of - overwhelm. Then, within that content, I share why it is they're overwhelmed, which brings them into the next phase.

Problem Aware Phase

Once an audience member realizes they have the problem you are helping to solve, they are in the problem-aware phase. They've felt a lightbulb moment go off and are relieved to know they aren't alone in the feelings they've been having. They're also open to hearing what you have to say about how they can solve their problem since you were the one that opened their eyes to what their problem was. You found their missing puzzle piece for them.

To continue using Content Batching Bootcamp as an example, now that my audience has realized their overwhelm with content comes from being stuck on the content creation hamster wheel and not having a system in place for creating, in their mind, they're asking, "what next?". So it's my job to begin to paint the picture of the solution for them, which is to create a batching system.

Solution Aware Phase

Now that your audience member is aware of the solution you've given them, they're likely starting to feel some overwhelm creeping in. After the endorphin rush of discovering that there's an answer to their problem dies down, they realize that in order to solve the problem, they still need to *do* something about it.

Which is where your offer comes in, right? Your offer is there to take the stress away and make it as simple as possible to implement the solution they're now aware will solve their problem. So it's time to tell them about your offer and why it's going to help.

With Content Batching Bootcamp, the course itself helps students craft a batching system that's unique to their business so that they can create a month's worth of content in one week - and say goodbye to the content creation hamster wheel. This pushes them into the offer-aware phase.

Offer Aware Phase

Finally, your audience is in the offer-aware phase. Not only are they aware of your offer, but by creating marketing around each phase of the customer journey, you've positioned your offer as *the* offer to solve their problem. Once someone is offer-aware, they're either going to purchase the offer and become a student/purchaser/client, or they will decide it's not the right fit for them.

Creating content for this phase of the customer journey means creating content around objections that someone might have to help them make the decision of whether or not your offer is the right fit for them.

Here are common objections to Content Batching Bootcamp and how I create content around them.

"I only work a few hours a week on my side hustle."

Content Batching Bootcamp was designed for the solopreneur, the side hustler, and the working mama. After working through the course, you'll have a custom system in place for creating a month's worth of content in just one week - whether you work forty hours or five.

"It takes me hours to create a single piece of content."

This comes down to one or two things - you're doing things the hard way, and/or you're a perfectionist. There's an entire lesson inside of Content Batching Bootcamp that will teach you how to stop spending hours on a single piece of content and start batching like a pro.

"I prefer to post in the moment when I'm feeling inspired."

Content creation can't happen without inspiration, but that doesn't mean you should stop what you're doing to create and post a piece of content just because you're feeling inspired. Inside Content Batching Bootcamp, I'll teach you how to capture and bottle those moments of inspiration while still saving a ton of time. This system is the best of both worlds.

After you've been selling your offer for a while, you'll begin to recognize common questions and patterns that arise that are objections that you'll need to address like these. Be sure to bake them into your content.

Student/Customer/Client Phase

After purchasing your offer, the customer journey is not complete. *Please* ensure that your offers guide your students/customers/clients through using and implementing the solution you've sold them. We won't go into details about that in this book because that doesn't fall under the umbrella of marketing, but I had to make that clear. We're ending your marketing customer journey here, but that is not the end of your full customer journey.

Once you've fleshed out your messaging for each phase of your customer journey, you'll have a handy cheat sheet to help create content that nurtures your audience. In fact, I created one for you, just print it and fill it out to keep handy for each of your offers. You can grab that at https://amandawarfield.com/customer-journey-cheat-sheet/

When you use content around each phase is dependent on whether you are live launching or using more evergreen sales funnels. If you're live launching, you'll want to breadcrumb out content, in phase order, in the eight to twelve weeks leading up to your launch. If you're using evergreen sales funnels, your funnel will walk them through the phases in order. In your content marketing, you'll want to make sure you're touching on each phase of the journey with your content, but it doesn't necessarily have to be in order because different audience members will always be in different phases, and the goal is to get them into your funnel so that you can move them through the customer journey.

Now that you know what phase of your business journey you're in and where you should be focusing your time and energy on your marketing, we need to talk about how to create effective marketing without allowing your marketing to take over your business.

Action Step:

Download and fill out the Customer Journey Cheat Sheet.
https://amandawarfield.com/customer-journey-cheat-sheet/

Additional Resources:

Chasing Simple Episode 132: Why Your Social Media Manager May Not Be
Getting the Results You're Looking For
https://amandawarfield.com/132-2/

KPI Tracker Template
https://amandawarfield.com/kpi-tracker/

For full resources in one place, head to:
https://amandawarfield.com/chasing-simple-marketing-bonuses/

SECTION 3
SIMPLIFY FOR CONSISTENCY

TEN

CONTENT IS NOT YOUR BUSINESS

How does this keep happening?

I was sitting in the dark at my desk. The house was quiet, and it was late - so late that in the back of my mind, I was counting down how many hours I had left to get some sleep before needing to get up and get to work teaching four-year-olds to read, get along, and sit for circle time. And all I was doing was staring at the blinking cursor on the blank page of a Word doc.

It was Sunday night, and my next blog post was supposed to be going live the next morning, but I couldn't think of anything to say. I had a topic and a title down, and that was about it. Being the granny that I am, it was about four hours past my bedtime, and all I wanted to do was walk across the hall and get in bed.

I saw two options left for me at this point: shut the laptop and give up on putting up a post for this week, or pull something out of my brain that was going to be mediocre at best just to put up something, *anything*. Either way, I knew I was doing a disservice to my audience.

So, I quickly pulled something out of my brain, typed it up onto the Word doc, transferred it to my website, and hit publish. It was already "tomorrow," anyway. Then I crawled into bed to try and get a couple of hours of sleep and promised myself that this was the last time this was going to happen. I was capital D-O-N-E.

And all of a sudden, it was Sunday again, and I was in the exact same place. Scrambling to put up something, *anything*, and either putting up nothing at all or putting out something low-quality. Neither of which help my business, and both of which might actually harm it.

It's so easy to push off your marketing. Tell yourself you'll get to it and then wind up at the very last second trying to throw something together. If this feels eerily familiar, you're stuck on the content creation hamster wheel. Even if you aren't creating, you're thinking about the need to create (at least in the back of your mind), which makes you feel guilty, and hangs over your head. You end up rushing through tasks so that you can hopefully rush through putting some kind of content out. Always rushing and always running on that wheel.

As soon as you get something posted, you're still not off of the wheel. Because now the countdown is on until the *next* time you're supposed to post something, and frankly, you're already stressed because you have no idea how you came up with what you just came up with. And now you've got to start thinking about something else.

It's time for you to jump off that hamster wheel my friend, so that you can show up both consistently *and* sustainably.

Dear reader, I need you to pay attention right now. If you've been skimming, stop and give me your full undivided attention for this next sentence, okay?

Ready?

Your content is part of your business, but it's not your entire business.

So please stop spending so much time and energy dealing with it.

Even if you're in the Content Creator phase right now and you haven't quite figured out what your business is going to look like. Creating content is not your entire business. You're likely learning, researching, brainstorming, connecting with others, and so much more. Don't let content creation take up all of your time and keep you stuck.

On the other hand, you will always need to market your business in some way, shape, or form. And maybe, in the end, you decide to market in ways outside of content marketing. But for so many of us, that's just not an option. Content marketing is a free to low-cost way to market our businesses, and we aren't going to be able to make the choice to stop utilizing it.

But the content creation hamster wheel? We also can't stay there forever. It's not sustainable. It's exhausting, overwhelming, creativity-sapping, and frankly, you're just not going to be putting out great content while you're on it.

But the most important factor when it comes to successfully seeing growth in your content marketing? Consistency.

Because consistently showing up in your marketing builds the Know, Like, and Trust factor. And as you'll recall, that Know, Like, and Trust factor is what builds relationships with your audience. When you build relationships with people, they'll start to:

- Engage with your content
- Share about your content and business with friends

- Become clients and students

All of this increases your growth - not only in your content marketing but also in your bottom line.

Consistency Builds Relationships

But we've got this dreaded problem that comes from the content creation hamster wheel - podfade.

Podfade is a common term used in the podcasting industry, and it's where you slowly fade out how often you're posting episodes until you eventually disappear altogether. This same thing happens across all types of content; podcasts are just the only ones that have a term for it at this point in time.

It happens so often because it's easy to decide to start showing up, creating content, and putting out podcast episodes (or insert other content types here). But once you get into it, you realize how time-consuming content creation is, and you end up overwhelmed and on that content creation hamster wheel. It no longer feels sustainable to put out episodes, so you decide to cut back on how many you're creating. Maybe you started with two a week, and you cut back to one. And at first, that helps. Wow! You've got so much extra time!

But slowly, the creep begins, and you begin to feel overwhelmed with that one episode a week. So you cut back to every other week and then maybe once a month. And eventually, you just decide to stop creating episodes altogether.

You've faded out.

In May 2022, Apple Podcasts hosted 2,450,689 different podcasts. Of those 2,450,689 podcasts, only 501,147 were considered active podcasts - 20.45%[6].

Apple qualifies a podcast as active if a new episode has been released in the last 90 days, so of those 501,147 in May of 2022 - it's safe to assume that not all of those are actually active.

Oh, and that 20.45%? That's down significantly from the 2021 numbers, in which 34% of the podcasts on Apple Podcasts were considered active[6].

But if you go back to 2018? Apple announced at its annual World-wide Developer Conference that there were 555,000 podcasts on their app, and over 525,000 of them were active[7] - so, roughly 94.59%.

Yes, as time goes on, there are plenty of podcasters that decide to end and retire their show, but they leave it up for the search engines and for people to continue to enjoy. However, many podcasters find themselves victims of podfade.

And this isn't just a podcaster problem. It happens across the board in all content channels. How often have you seen a creator pop onto their social media and say, "Hey! I'm back! Sorry, I was MIA; life got busy!"

Probably only about a hundred times, right?

Please. I'm begging you. Do not do this. Because if they didn't miss you, now they know you ghosted them. Just hop back in. Note: when it comes to your long-form content and your email newsletter, I would say definitely give an explanation, but not social media. It's so chaotic, and they probably didn't notice you were gone.

Fading out with your content is so easy to do once you're stuck on that content creation hamster wheel. No matter the format.

What happens to your audience when you fade out? Let's say you have a favorite podcast, YouTube channel, or blog, and you always check in on the newest content on a specific day of the week.

Maybe it's a favorite podcast, and every Wednesday a new episode comes out. And every Wednesday morning, on the way to work, you tune into that new episode. Only one Wednesday, you go to listen, and there's no new episode. You're a little bummed, but you think, "Maybe there's a tech glitch, I'll try again on the way home." So you turn on a different podcast and make your way to work. And when you get in the car to head home at the end of the day, you try to put on that new episode again and again, no new episode.

So you check back the next day, and the next, and maybe again the next Wednesday to see if there was maybe one this time. But pretty soon, you've gotten into another podcast and filled your Wednesday morning drive with it.

Then, suddenly, a few months down the road, they pop back up. You've got a notification that there's a new episode. Do you immediately start listening? Maybe. Maybe you turn it on immediately hoping for an explanation. Maybe you get one, and maybe you don't. But either way, you've got a new routine. While you're not purposefully *not* going to listen anymore, it just potentially won't happen as naturally. Now you've got to fit this podcast back into your routines, and maybe there's a part of you in the back of your mind wondering if they're just going to disappear again for a few months.

It felt like those podcast hosts were your friends, and they completely ghosted you. You might as well have made a coffee date that they didn't show up to for all the heads-up they gave you about going silent for a few months. Now you aren't sure what to expect from them.

And if they ghost you more than once? That slight miffed feeling immediately sends them into flaky friend territory. You know, like that one friend you have that you make plans with, but you never actually count on the plans happening because something always comes up? That's who these hosts are to you now. You still enjoy the podcast, and you still like them. But you also don't see yourself relying on them again.

I hear your thoughts right now, friend.

"Great. Thanks, Amanda. I picked up this book for help, not to feel worse about myself."

The good news is that there's a way to fix it. Being consistent with your content. Being inconsistent may undermine your relationships with your audience and all of the work you're doing, but consistency will grow those relationships. It further solidifies that Know, Like, and Trust factor. Not to mention, showing up consistently will also help create consistent messaging and help you see consistent growth (even though it's *not* a growth strategy 😌).

Consistency Hones Messaging

I adore my clients. There's never been a single client that I've worked with that I didn't absolutely love working with. And for that, I am so grateful.

You see when I'm working one-on-one with clients, we meet at the end of each quarter to prepare their content marketing strategy for the quarter ahead. We review their goals, review their calendar, determine upcoming promotions and launches, create plans for those, review their messaging, and then we dive into the strategy for the content itself. And for each piece of content they're going to create, I help them strategize what the topic will be, what the call to action will be, and what their hook should be.

They walk away with a fully strategized content plan, and all they have to do is create the content. The beauty is that I help hone the strategy and messaging and tell them exactly what to talk about and when - and all they have to do is talk about it.

But, I've had clients that will end their call with me excited and motivated to take the plan we came up with and start creating. And they'll get the first few pieces created and put out into the world. And then they'll get busy, forget to post, and when they show back up for our next meeting, I essentially have to send them into the world with the same content plan. Sure, we tweak it based on what's coming up on their calendar, but we did all that work to come up with the best possible plan, and they didn't implement it. And because they didn't implement it, I have no data or information to see how it performed.

In Chapters Seven, Eight, and Nine, I shared how you can begin incorporating content marketing strategy at various phases of your business. And all those strategies are great, but only if you use them. When my clients don't actually implement the strategy we created, we can't make improvements to their messaging because we have no feedback. We don't know how it landed, if anything really jumped at their audience, or if anything completely flopped.

Which is why I eventually began to offer copywriting services to my clients as well. You can spend weeks coming up with what you believe to be the best messaging in the world, but without showing up and sharing that messaging - it means nothing. And it does nothing for you.

Typically, when my clients come to me, they believe that their biggest issue with content marketing is that they don't have a plan and they want some direction. However, on a deeper level, their real issue is a lack of consistency - one that leads to incoherent messaging.

Remember the problem unaware to problem aware journey? That's exactly what's coming into play here. One recent client, Sydney, told me that her hope in working with me was that she would walk away with a well-laid-out plan for her marketing and that she would feel confident that she was doing her best to call in her ideal clients - all with feelings of peace and ease around her marketing efforts.

Sadly, I just had to say goodbye to Sydney as a client, but for the absolute best reason. Over our year of working together, she had found so much peace and ease with her content that she no longer felt she needed my support. Because we spent hours of our time together digging into her messaging, and over our year, she reiterated her phrasing of her messaging over and over again until it felt right. With each session, we'd peel back more layers, and by the end, she was confident in what she was sharing - which made her content a breeze to plan and create.

Consistently showing up? That forces you to share that messaging and re-share it. And see how your audience reacts to it. Not every piece of content will be a hit. Most will perform just okay, in fact. But every now and then, you'll get a piece of content that really takes off. And once it does, you can reuse that messaging. You can repurpose that content. And you can continue moving forward with improved messaging because now you know what connected with your audience.

But without consistency? You aren't showing up enough to measure that impact, *and* you aren't building strong relationships, so even if some of your messaging hits, your audience may not feel comfortable telling you that.

This is one more reason it's so important to be consistent with your content.

Consistency Aids Growth

I was sitting at my friend's dining room table, sipping coffee and enjoying the beautiful Washington skyline through their massive windows. Their second child had been born a few weeks prior, and I'd flown out to lend a hand however I could now that her husband was back at work. It was November, which in my business is an extremely busy season of preparing for Black Friday, and also filling my client spots for the next year. This meant that I was getting up long before everyone else in order to get a little work done before the day became full.

This one particular morning, I booted up my laptop and opened my email to discover a new client inquiry sitting inside. Now, as I mentioned a second ago, this was at the height of signing clients for the new year, so having a client inquiry in my inbox wasn't exactly surprising.

However, this client inquiry in and of itself *was* a surprise because we hadn't had a single conversation about working together yet. With almost every client, before they fill out my inquiry form on my website, we tend to have conversations through social media direct messaging to talk through whether or not they're a good fit. It's not required, of course, but typically clients feel more confident going into a working relationship this way. In fact, I do the same thing. If I'm thinking of hiring someone, I'll usually reach out with a few questions first before filling out their contact form.

I immediately sent my brochure, and within the hour, she'd signed her contract and paid her deposit. And the way she came to decide to work with me? Through my podcast. She'd been listening to episode after episode, and when she heard me sharing about client spaces there, she decided it was the right fit. Without those episodes going up on a consistent basis, I wouldn't have been nurturing this potential lead so well, and I wouldn't have seen that growth in my business.

When it comes to growth through your content, there are two types of growth - direct and indirect.

Direct Growth

I was lying in bed, waking up, and I reached over to my phone to pull it off the charger. I was stuck in our guest room, quarantining thanks to Covid, and all of my routines were out the window. So, I figured, why not start my day by checking my inbox? I swiped over to the last screen on my phone, and I tapped that little Gmail app open. And right there on top was an email whose subject line read:

"Your podcast has made the Goodpods Top 100 Charts!"

In my just-woken-up and groggy-from-Covid state, my first thought was, "Huh?". I immediately clicked on it and couldn't believe what I was seeing. *My* podcast, Chasing Simple, was actually ranked on somebody's charts?. There's absolutely no way. But sure enough, here's what the email said:

Congratulations!

Chasing Simple has made the following top listener charts on Goodpods:

#20 in the Top 100 Entrepreneurship chart
#21 in the Top 100 Self-Improvement chart
#46 in the Top 100 Business chart

You could have knocked me over with a feather.

Number 20 in the Entrepreneurship chart?! Number 46 in the Business chart?! I pulled open the Goodpods app and scrolled around and couldn't believe the podcasts that I was sitting next to in the charts. Business owners I'd long admired. Entrepreneurs that felt "legit" while I still felt like I was playing pretend sometimes. Right there beside my podcast. Even below my podcast, in some cases. It was unreal.

My very first month of podcasting? I had just 730 downloads. And that wasn't one or two episodes with 730 downloads. It was EIGHT. 730 downloads through eight episodes means that, on average, there were 91 downloads of each episode. Less than 100 listens per episode.

And now, here I was, just over 100 episodes later, and I was getting an email saying my podcast was in the top 100 listener charts on this app.

It was one of those "Wow, I can't believe this is happening" moments. But, at the same time, I'd been at it for 116 episodes at this point. More than two years of consistently showing up and putting out a new episode week after week after week. Years of building that Know, Like, and Trust factor with my audience. Even when I didn't want to. Even when I thought that no one was listening. Even when I felt like I was never going to make any growth or progress, I kept showing up and putting those episodes out. And those download numbers showed direct growth in my content, as each month new listeners found the show, and I could measure that growth.

The same is true for everyone's content. The longer you consistently show up, the more downloads, subscribers, views, followers, etc., you'll have. Does that mean the growth will happen quickly? Definitely not. Does that mean that your only form of growing your business should be content growth? You already know the answer based on the previous chapters where we've discussed growth strategies in depth. But will your content audience grow over time if you consistently show up? Yes, absolutely. And the larger the audience, the more people you have to nurture and bring into your business.

Indirect Growth

"My revenue has increased over twice from last year. Yes, there are a lot of factors, but I think related to our work together - the confidence I got working with you and leaning into my authentic voice in my marketing was crucial to my growth."

Remember Sydney - the client I recently said goodbye to that was now feeling so confident and peaceful in her marketing? This is part of the testimonial she sent in about working together. Over the last year, she's seen incredible growth in her business. Not only did she double her revenue, but she's at the point where she's having to turn away clients and reconsider her business model. All while enjoying the clients she's working with and making space for her husband to start his own business as well. It's been incredible to watch.

And as she mentions in the testimonial, none of that is directly related to the content she's been putting out. In fact, she was putting out the fewest volume of content of any of my clients. A blog post or two a month, one email newsletter, and a few social media posts. None of that content was necessarily directly bringing in her dream clients.

But even though she didn't have a large volume of content, and she wasn't seeing direct growth through that content, there were still plenty of factors at play from the work we were doing together.

She was putting out quality content consistently. Small volume but high quality. It truly does make a difference. And the fact that she was diving into her messaging played out in many ways. It created a cohesive content ecosystem. So when someone found her online, they immediately understood what she did and whether or not she could help them with their particular problem. It also made it possible for her to show up confidently for her business in all other areas. Once she understood exactly who she was speaking to, who she wanted to work with, and how she wanted to help them, it was much easier for her to take steps forward in her business without feeling cluttered. She could show up and move the needle in a way that was conducive to growing her business *and* feeling confident about how she was serving others.

Was this growth measurable and directly related to her content? No. There's no way to pick a number to definitively show that any of her growth was related to her content or what we were doing together. But can it indirectly be related to her content? I believe so, and based on her testimonial, so does she.

For myself and Sydney (and my other clients), consistency paid off. And it will continue to pay off. But it does take showing up, even when it's not easy. Even when you don't want to, and it takes time. Remember how we talked about patience back in Chapter Two? That's where this comes in. In order to see growth, you've got to get started, you've got to build relationships, and you've got to be consistent. It often takes time to see the fruits of your labor, but if you give yourself that time - good things are going to grow.

Be honest with me for a minute, friend. Did you read all of that and think, "Great. Consistency. Consistency improves my relationships with my audience. Consistency improves my messaging. Consistency aids growth. The problem is I'm overwhelmed, Amanda. I'm the one sitting in front of that blinking cursor in the middle of the night. I understand the importance of consistency. But HOW? How do I get consistent?"

Oh, my dear, I'm so glad you asked.

Consistency with your content doesn't need to be so overwhelming, time-consuming, and complicated. In fact, you might say that it's quite... *Simple*. In order to show up consistently, you've got to simplify your content creation process. I've got three steps to help you do just that. Simplify your content creation to avoid the content creation overwhelm, stop ghosting your audience, and start showing up consistently without sacrificing your time or mental energy. We'll talk in detail about each of them in the next three chapters.

Action Step:

It's time to create another important reminder for yourself. Take out a piece of paper and write: "Consistency ≠ Constant". You'll be glad to have this reminder in front of you as we dive into the next three chapters.

Additional Resources:

Chasing Simple Episode 042: My Schedule for Creating Consistent Content
https://amandawarfield.com/042-2/

For full resources in one place, head to:
https://amandawarfield.com/chasing-simple-marketing-bonuses/

ELEVEN
CREATE LESS CONTENT

I grew up in sunny South Carolina, in a tiny town that you've probably never heard of. And while most people who live here complain all summer long about the heat and the humidity and then complain all winter long about not getting a "real" winter or ever seeing snow ... I *loved* it.

I love the heat that makes it necessary to spend your summer days at the pool or lake. I love the humidity that feels like the air is wrapping you in a great big hug. I love the summer storms that come in loud and fierce but end as quickly as they begin - leaving the sun to do its thing and create even more humidity with all the buckets of rain that hit the ground. I love being able to skate by in the winter, barely needing a jacket. I never in a million years imagined any plan outside of graduating high school, heading off to attend the University of South Carolina, and then marrying a hometown boy and coming right back.

We all know that saying about making plans and God laughing, right?

Turns out, I did go to USC. And I did marry a hometown boy. The only thing missing? I most definitely did not come right back.

When I met my husband, he was about to ship off for boot camp. We were lucky that his very first duty station was in South Carolina, but two years after we were married, he received orders for his brand new duty station - out in Washington State.

We moved out to Washington that Memorial Day weekend, and by the beginning of August, Russell was out on his first deployment. And, whew. When the rainy season hit that October, I was not prepared. Because here's the thing about the rain (at least in the part of Washington we were in), it's not rain like I knew back home. In South Carolina, when it rains, it *rains*. It pours, it's loud, it thunders, there's lightning, and then it's over. But not in Washington. Nope. It just *mists*. All day. Every day. Every damn day. Mist, clouds, and cold from September through April, and then it gets just warm enough to *maybe* not need a cardigan in the summer.

I was exhausted. I was teaching three classes between two different preschools, one of which was a start-up where I had also been hired as the director. I was very involved with my church and the youth group. I was a mentor for the sorority I had been in during college. Not to mention I was, in general, trying to do everything to manage a household by myself and try and make it through six months without my husband, all the way across the country from everyone and everything I knew.

So, I started drinking coffee.

And then I started drinking more. Then, the weather started getting to me, so I began drinking even more. And all of a sudden, I was drinking coffee all day long, every day. If I walked into the church in the evening *without* a travel mug in my hand, somebody had a comment to make.

And here's the thing about coffee. We all know and can agree that the best coffee is cups with fun flavors, whipped cream on top, and maybe even a sprinkle of cinnamon or a swirl of caramel, right? But when I was drinking coffee all day, I couldn't afford that many Starbucks trips, and I wasn't going to make fancy coffee for myself that many times a day. I was stumbling to my Ninja in the morning, scooping the grinds into the machine and having it spit out Plain Jane coffee as quickly as possible before I poured some creamer and sucked it down. That was all I had the time and mental capacity for.

Then, somehow three and a half years had miraculously passed in the blink of an eye, and it was time for us to move back to South Carolina, where the sun, humidity, mild winters, and short rains welcomed us home. All of a sudden, I didn't feel quite like I needed to drink coffee all day long. Two cups were usually more than enough, and when I felt tired, I'd get outside and walk around in the sun for a bit. Wild how that works to perk you up.

We even started to buy things like whipped cream, caramel drizzle, and syrups, and especially in the fall and winter would doctor up our coffee and make it fancy. Because we had the time. We had the mental capacity. No longer were we making and drinking coffee all day, but instead, it became almost like a treat, and we were more inclined to make higher-quality cups.

And the same is true for your content.

If you're focused on putting out a ton of content just for the sake of putting out content, you're more than likely watering down the content you're putting out. You aren't giving your audience your best work.

When you have the time and mental capacity to create content without feeling rushed, you're much more likely to be able to take some time to create high-quality content. The kind that makes people pay attention, the kind that builds relationships with your audience, and the kind that moves your business forward. Sort of like when I'm not drinking coffee all day long, I can take it slow and create a fancy cup of coffee to sip on and enjoy.

But how do you make the time and mental capacity to create that high-quality content? You create better content less often.

Amanda, you've spent this entire book telling me I need to show up consistently. And now you're saying to show up less? What gives?

Oh, my sweet, sweet friend. Yes, you need to show up consistently. But here's the truth: you do not need to show up constantly to be consistent.

Showing up consistently means showing up when expected. And **you** get to set those expectations, my friend. So if you decide you only want to put up long-form content once a month? Just make sure you're putting out that content at the same time every month so that your audience knows when to expect more from you.

For example, both of these would be considered consistent content:

One blog post is posted on the first of the month, every month.

One blog post is posted on Monday, every Monday.

Both are consistent; one is just slightly more constant than the other.

So, instead of trying to show up everywhere, all the time - start showing up *less*.

If you just felt a moment of panic, I get it. When you started learning about content marketing, one of the things you probably Googled was "How many times should you post on social media a week?" or "How often should you write blog posts?". And you probably got told some very high number that would be considered best practice, and you've been trying to keep up ever since - never being able to step off of that content creation hamster wheel.

Here's the thing. When it comes to the best practices surrounding how often you're "supposed" to create content, they're simply best practices. In some regard, it's a numbers game, like the whole numbers on the email list and conversion rates - the more followers, the more sales. The more posts, the more likely you are to be seen.

BUT. You do not have to post according to best practices to see growth. Would you grow faster if you did? Sure. But it's not going to be sustainable, and you'll become that flaky friend that no one trusts completely, which will stunt your growth significantly more than if you just slowed down and chose a speed you could handle. The turtle beats the hare and all of that.

I also want you to stop and consider the educators and influencers you follow that seem able to keep up with best practices. Now take a moment to think about how many team members they have. Even if you don't know the exact number, I'm guessing it's more than you have. Those creators can create the basics of their content and then pass it off to have it finalized by other team members, which means they can create significantly more content in less time and keep it high-quality.

You may not be there yet. But one day you might, so keep that in mind. Start with a sustainable amount of content, and over time, feel free to bump it up to more. But start smaller than you think you need to. Our goal is to simplify as much as possible to show up consistently.

In order to do that, you're going to want to cut back on two things: where you're showing up and how often you're showing up.

Where You're Showing Up

First, make a list of all of the different types of content you're creating. All of the platforms you're using. And, if you're creating more than one type of content within a platform, write each of those down as its own "platform" as well.

Then, cut down on how many platforms you're showing up on. There's no reason for you to show up on every single platform. And if we can simplify how many different places you're trying to show up, we'll be able to free up a ton of time.

Podcast
YouTube
Email Newsletter
Social Media 1
Social Media 2
Social Media 3

→

~~Podcast~~
(YouTube)
(Email Newsletter)
~~Social Media~~ 1
(Social Media 2)
~~Social Media~~ 3

→

YouTube
Email Newsletter
Social Media 2

My rule of thumb is to have one type of long-form content, an email newsletter, and one type of social media. If that feels like too much, start with an email newsletter and one type of social media. If that feels like too little, remember - you can always add on later. We're starting small, getting off the content creation hamster wheel, getting consistent, and then upping our game. And don't forget; this is just a starting point. At some point, you'll likely be able to outsource parts of your creation process, allowing you to create more content.

Need help determining where exactly you should be showing up? Here's a refresher from the advice in Chapter One:

> You might be wondering which types of content are suitable for you. You're interested in starting to create long-form content but aren't sure where. You want to get serious about social media but are overwhelmed by all of the platforms. How do you choose?

> For long-form content, there are three things you should consider:

> - Your personality type.
> - The amount of time you have for content creation.
> - What your content is about and the best way to present it.

Which Type of Long-Form Content is for You?

BLOG	PODCAST	YOUTUBE
Great for Introverts	Great for Introverts and Extroverts	Great for Extroverts
Least Amount of Time to Create	More Time Consuming than a Blog, but Less than YouTube	Most Amount of Time to Create
Great for Content that Can be Explained by Written Word, or a Graphic/Image	Great for Content that Doesn't Need Visuals	Great for Content that is Best Shown Visually

Are you more introverted and prefer to be behind the scenes? A blog or a podcast might be the best choice for you.

Are you more extroverted? A podcast or a YouTube channel might be the best bet.

Yes, a podcast is excellent for both introverts and extroverts, thanks to how customizable it is. For the extreme introverts, you can podcast using only solo episodes you record by yourself or guest episodes without cameras. On the other hand, for extreme extroverts, you can podcast mainly with guest episodes and your camera on, giving you the joy of interacting with others.

Ask yourself which type calls to you the most. That's the one you'll want to lean into.

However, you'll also want to consider how much time you *actually* have to create content. YouTube videos will take up much more of your time than a podcast, and a blog will take up the least time.

Of course, if you're passionate about video but hate writing - in theory, a blog post could take you longer than a YouTube video. You'll also need to consider that when thinking over your available time.

And a final consideration would be the type of content you will create. You might not want to go the podcast route if it's heavily visual. However, a podcast might be perfect if it's not that visual.

When we see and hear someone talking, we tend to form relationships with them faster than if we were reading a blog post they wrote. So, a podcast will build relationships with your audience more quickly than a blog, and a Youtube channel will build relationships faster than a podcast. But when you're at a stage in business, your primary consideration should be your time availability. So, there's no right or wrong answer when it comes to which type of long-form content you put out. Ask yourself those three questions, and see where they lead you.

As far as social media goes, there are two things you'll want to consider:

1. Where is your audience?
2. Where do you enjoy showing up?

Earlier, I said that your marketing isn't about you. And it's not. At the same time, if you're only showing up on one social media platform, it might as well be one you enjoy. Because if you hate it, you won't spend time creating content for that platform, which makes showing up there pointless.

However, consider who your audience is and where they spend their time. If you do not want to show up on a particular platform, but it's the best place to reach your audience? You might want to consider a trial run to see if you get more into it than expected.

How do you find your people? Age can play an essential role in determining where they might be. Let's face it; various generations use content marketing differently. Again, so as not to age this book prematurely, I won't get into who is where specifically, but considering age should give you considerable insight into where your people are.

We want to make sure that we're showing up where our audience is showing up - otherwise, how will we get in front of them? Simply showing up and creating content isn't enough; you've got to be the one to find them using growth strategies. Remember, if you build it, they will *not* come.

But we also want to enjoy creating content because marketing should be fun. So what kind of content is the easiest and most enjoyable for you to create?

If the platform you enjoy creating content for conflicts with where your audience is consuming content, I suggest starting with where your clients are and trying to learn how to make it fun. If you spend some months hating it, add a content stream that you enjoy to help the creativity flow.

How Often You're Showing Up

After you've decided where you will stop showing up and where you will continue to show up, write out how often you're trying to show up at each place you're going to continue with. How many times a week are you creating and posting content for that type?

Then, cut that down. In fact, cut it in half. Why half? Everyone has different amounts of capacity, and creating content takes various amounts of time for different people. While it would be great to give you an exact number to start with, I've found that this cut it in half method has worked repeatedly for the hundreds of students that have gone through my program, Content Batching Bootcamp.

As humans, we are prone to overestimating our abilities to get things done and also underestimating how long any given task will take. Therefore, if you cut down your amount of content by half, you'll have a strong starting point for moving forward at a sustainable level.

CREATE LESS CONTENT

Per Month	Per Month	Per Month
4 YouTube Videos	2 YouTube Videos	2 YouTube Videos
4 Email Newsletters	2 Email Newsletters	2 Email Newsletters
20 Social Media 2 Posts	10 Social Media 2 Posts	10 Social Media 2 Posts

You do not need to put out as much content as you think you do, and two high-quality YouTube videos each month will do more for your marketing than four that are mediocre or worse.

My caveat is that if you take a ton of time creating your content because you're a perfectionist, it's not cutting back on the amount you're posting that will help. Two great YouTube videos a month will do *significantly* more for your business than one perfect video each month. You need to focus on not letting perfection stand in the way.

If that's where you're struggling and where all of your time is going, you need to set boundaries with yourself on how much time you're allowed to spend editing each piece of content. If you can't enforce that - I highly recommend seriously considering investing in outsourcing the editing.

Like with my coffee, if you spend less time creating content, you'll have more energy to get creative with what you are putting out. The bottom line is that instead of trying to show up everywhere, all of the time, the first way to help get consistent with your content is by showing up *less*. You don't need to put out as much content as you think you do as long as you're showing up consistently and listening to your audience.

Action Step:

Cut down on how many platforms you're showing up on and then how often you're showing up on each.

Additional Resources:

Chasing Simple Episode 014: Creating Consistent Content
https://amandawarfield.com/014-2/

For full resources in one place, head to:
https://amandawarfield.com/chasing-simple-marketing-bonuses/

TWELVE
BECOME A BROKEN RECORD

My best friend Molly has sunshine in her DNA, I'm convinced. She is the warmest, happiest person I know. The Enneagram Seven to my One. Always up for an adventure. She is always down to listen to me cry on the phone over my business - and she's not even an entrepreneur. (You know how rare it is to find this.) Molly's a hands-on mom and always has sensory bins and interactive activities for her two boys to do. She won't mind me saying that she's a clean freak because she's proud of it (as she should be - her home is always spotless), yet when her two-year-old took a piece of black chalk to their cream-colored couch? Molly laughed, encouraged him, and sent me a picture. I'm sure that as soon as the boys were in bed, she scrubbed the heck out of the couch, but at the moment, she just let him be happy, knowing he wasn't harming anything. That's just the kind of person she is.

And yet, when I think of Molly. None of that is what I think of first. When I think of Molly, my first thought is always "California."

Why? Molly is from California and talks about it whenever she can fit it into a conversation.

The weather, the Mexican food, In-and-Out (Sorry Mols, I will never get on board with In-and-Out being even mildly comparable to Five Guys), the beaches, all of the fun things to do. If she can fit it into the conversation, she will.

And it's not that she's trying to do that purposely. She's probably not even consciously aware that she's doing it. She just really loves her home state and loves to talk about it. It's part of who she is.

But now, in my mind, Molly and California are linked forever. If I think Molly, I think of California. And if I think of California, I think of Molly. If I ever need to visit California, I immediately tell her and ask for her recommendations. When something makes me think of California, I'll send her a picture because I know she'll get it. It's her thing.

But this connection didn't happen the first time we met. In fact, when we first met, she'd come into my classroom to give me a bathroom break, and sit down on one of the tiny kids' chairs, and ask me questions about myself with a massive smile on her face and my first thought was "wow, she's really nice."

It didn't happen the second time we met.

And it didn't happen the first time we hung out outside of work when we went out on her and her husband's boat, and Russell got sunburned, but we went home happy because not only does Molly have sunshine in her DNA, but so does Ethan and it's impossible not to be happy around the two of them.

It didn't happen the second, third, or fourth time we hung out.

But slowly, over time, because she talked about California consistently, I realized that Molly and California would forever be linked in my mind.

When it comes to your content, you want your audience to link you in their mind with what you're an expert at. You want them to think, "Oh. {Your Name}? Yeah, they {your area of expertise}." And vice versa. You want to be the first thing that pops into their brain when they think of what you're an expert in.

And yet, how many times have you ever thought, "I need to come up with something new and fresh to share with my audience?"

We want to keep things fresh and exciting, but in reality, if we hop around from topic to topic to topic (ahem - like in the bucket strategy), our audience is going to have no idea what it is that we do. You must teach them if you want them to think {your area of expertise}. Which means you have to tell them - over and over again.

Think about it from their perspective. Even if you're posting new content every single day, each audience member is only going to see a small fraction of what it is that you're putting out there. I tried to research what that percentage of organic reach currently was for social media and found many different claims (Anywhere from 1% to 25%), and no one cited where those numbers came from. Not to mention that this is constantly changing with new updates.

I was chatting with someone recently, and they asked how my business was doing. At one point, they said they were concerned I'd shut it down because they hadn't seen my posts in a while when they used to see them all the time. And it all comes down to that algorithm. So, I'll leave it at this - a tiny fraction of people see a small fraction of what you post.

(Hence my earlier urging you to have long-form content and an email newsletter as well as social media.)

But, if a small fraction of what you put out there is being seen, think about how many times you'd need to post about the same topic before it even began to set in. I don't have a number for you, but it's a LOT. If you've ever heard of the Marketing Rule of Seven[8], you'll know that it says that we need to see something seven to ten times before we take action on it, which means you need to take whatever number you thought you needed for expert awareness posting and multiply it by ten. You can't post about something once or twice and expect people to think you're an expert in that area. It has to be all you ever talk about.

And then you *might* be connected in their mind as the expert in what you do.

Which is why I urge you to refrain from trying and keeping things fresh and new. Your audience doesn't want fresh and new; they want more of what you're already saying. YOU want fresh and new, but your content marketing isn't for you.

You want fresh and new, but your content marketing is not for you.

This is especially true as you are becoming established as a business owner in the Foundation Builder phase. Stick to one clear topic until you know you've established yourself as an expert. This takes time, but in the end, you'll see faster growth than if you were all over the place because you didn't want to pigeonhole yourself into one topic. I promise it doesn't have to be like that forever. Once you're established, you can start focusing on fresh ways to say the same thing. If you've got a firm grip on your messaging, you'll get new ideas from your audience members about how they phrase things - giving you that ability to reframe things in a "fresh" way.

Constantly giving your audience something new and fresh is doing yourself, your business, and your audience a disservice. If they don't know how you can help, they won't be buying from you and won't be able to share about you with others when someone is looking for an expert like you.

But Amanda. I'm bored. It's hard to create content around something I'm bored of.

To which I say - you may not be passionate enough to make money in this area if you're too bored to talk about it repeatedly.

However, if your biggest roadblock isn't so much that you're bored but more so that you're uncertain what else people want to hear from you, that's a different story. It's time to become a broken record, my friend.

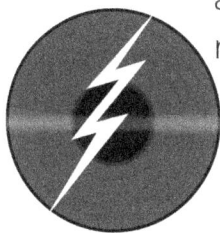

Become a broken record

Keep talking about the same topic repeatedly, and when you get tired of talking about it, talk about it some more. Once people believe you're the expert you say you are, they will start asking questions. And when they start asking questions, you will have even more content ideas to create.

And how does this save time and help you show up consistently?

Well, if you aren't constantly having to come up with new things to talk about and are instead talking about the same thing repeatedly, there's a fun little trick you can use - repurposing your content.

Repurposing Creates Consistency

Taking content you've already created and reusing it in new ways helps you be a broken record and become an expert; it saves you a ton of time and mental energy that would otherwise be used trying to come up with new things to say.

Not to mention, we spend a large chunk of time creating long-form content. We want to ensure it works for us for much longer than we spend working on it.

How many times have you created a piece of long-form content - spent hours on it - and mentioned it all of one time to your audience? Maybe you put up a post on social media about it, and then you told your email newsletter, and after that, you never thought about it again? You were already on to the next piece of long-form content - drafting, creating, scheduling, and barely remembering to share about it before hopping onto the next one.

Let's say you spend about four hours creating long-form content from start to finish. And repurposing said content into two pieces of short-form content takes about thirty minutes. If you only ever post about your long-form content right when it releases, with those two posts, you've only spent an eighth of the time it took you to create it to promote it. Next time you're creating content, time how long each piece takes you - because you want to promote each piece of content for more time than you spent creating it. Especially considering how little of your content gets seen thanks to the algorithm.

You should spend more time
promoting your content
than you do creating it.

Our goal is to spend more time sharing about a piece of long-form content than we do creating it. Because the more you share, the more eyes you get on that piece of content, and the more you see growth. So, we're going to make the most of your time, showcase yourself as the expert, and start showing up consistently by repurposing and reusing your written, audio, video, and social media content.

Repurposing Written Content

Repurposing written content is the easiest of the three (written, audio, video) because you can literally copy and paste to present it as a new type of written content. You can turn a blog post into an email or a social media post. You can turn a blog post into audio or video content by using what was written previously to record a podcast episode or Youtube video. You can even take a blog post and turn it into part of a book, course, or some other paid offer.

The best way to showcase exactly how I repurpose content is by taking an old blog post and doing it for you on these pages. So, first, the blog post:

Time Blocking For Beginners

I am constantly looking for new ways to manage my time better because I want to get done what needs to be done, but I also want to make sure I have time to tend to myself. Time Blocking has made me more productive and also less frazzled.

What is Time Blocking?

Time Blocking is a type of scheduling that will help you manage your time better. There are two different schools of thought when it comes to Time-Blocking. The first is working by your task, not by the clock.

With this method, you determine your tasks for the day and then work on them until they are complete. Once they're done, you're done working for the day. So if you decide that your tasks are running to the bank, doing a load of laundry, and baking cupcakes for the upcoming bake sale, and you get all that done before noon, then hey, you're done for the day. Typically, if this type of schedule works for you, you wake up motivated to face the day and finish your tasks as soon as possible.

However, I align myself with the second school of thought regarding Time Blocking. I'm a procrastinator and a recovering perfectionist, which means if I follow this school of thought, I will sit there and spend entirely too long working on those cupcakes. I'll make sure they look just so and are perfectly decorated. Or, I'll put off my tasks until the end of the day because, hey, it's only three things, and then end up scrambling at the end of the night and feeling overwhelmed, which defeats the entire purpose of me bothering to Time Block anyways.

I follow the clock when I Time Block my day. That way, I can focus on progress, not perfection. This forces me to not procrastinate-I have to start projects with ample time in advance in order to have enough time to get them done, and also to only spend so long working on something.

For example, this morning, I set aside two hours to work on writing blog posts. Every 25 minutes, I'll get up and walk around and clear my mind for 5 minutes (more on this later in this post), and then I get right back to work. I'll work until those two hours are up, and then it's time to move on to my next block. Whether I finished my tasks or not. By starting far in advance, I can always schedule a new time block for that task the next day. I like to do it this way because I'm an over-scheduler—every single time. I'm working on it, but inevitably, I always assume I can get more done than I actually can.

So you can decide which style works best for you-blocking by the clock or by the tasks.

Why Should You Use Time Blocking?

Besides the fact that it can help you avoid procrastination and can majorly increase your productivity (there are claims that this one thing can increase your productivity by 150%), Time Blocking can also help you take control of your time. It shows you where you're being unrealistic and where you're spending your day. It helps you effectively organize your time and also enables you to focus on your task at hand at each moment.

As you continue in your Time Blocking journey, you'll be able to answer the age-old question of "Where did the time go?". Even though your day will rarely go exactly as planned, it helps to give you a much better picture of where you are spending your time. Then you can continue to adjust and make tweaks.

When I first started Time Blocking, I wasn't scheduling any time to eat or rest in the middle of the day. At first, I assumed that my commute from the preschool to my house would be enough of a mental break that I could immediately pick up working on the blog and work for a few hours. I learned quickly that I had an unrealistic expectation here and started to build in 30 minutes of downtime between school and blog work. It's made a world of difference in my attitude and productivity, and if I hadn't been Time Blocking out my day, I don't think I would have realized it on a conscious level. Most likely, I would have just ended up taking a break anyways, getting lost on social media or in a book, and then getting in bed wondering where the day had gone and why I had not achieved my goals.

Not only that but in working towards being more intentional, I want to make sure I'm setting aside time for the things that matter. It is so easy to put ourselves and our relationships on the back burner behind our to-do lists. We tell ourselves that if we keep going and finish these tasks, we'll have time to relax. But **that will never be the case.** There will always be something else to do. There will always be a next task. Blocking out my day helps me to purposefully plan time for my priorities and block out the rest of the noise of life.

The Pomodoro Method of Time Blocking

Francesco Cirillo came up with this method in 1992, based on his use of a tomato timer he had. The key feature of this method is the batching of similar tasks within a 25-minute block. After each 25-minute block, there is a 5-minute break. After four twenty-five-minute blocks, you'll take a longer 15-30 minute break.

Batching helps you to focus and minimize distractions because you are grouping similar tasks together and not having to jump from one task to a completely different task. Otherwise, your brain would slow down with every refocus on other tasks.

Cirillo used 25 minutes because it's long enough to get something done but short enough that you can stay hyper-focused and productive. Trying to concentrate for much longer than that will lead to burnout.

So when it's time to get to work, set a timer for 25 minutes, and don't allow distractions to pull you out of your groove. After that timer goes off, take a 5-minute break. I prefer to get up and walk around because it rejuvenates me and helps me to be ready to focus for the next 25 minutes. Working at a computer, I often find myself with a slight headache/tension at the end of my block. Then I use those 5 minutes to walk around and do mindless things like picking up this pillow, folding this blanket, etc., which helps clear my mind of the tension.

How to Time Block

Alright, now it's time to start Time Blocking for yourself. First, look at your non-negotiables. What are the things you can't negotiate? Such as school drop-off and pick-up, work, gym schedule, church, etc. You should also be including white space for yourself in your non-negotiables. I know it's always the first thing to sacrifice, but you can't serve others well if your well is dry. Make sure you're making time for yourself to rejuvenate.

Next, you have to determine your big goals. What are your priorities? What goals surround your priorities? What other plans do you have, or what projects do you want to work on?

Break those big goals down into smaller steps. What are your monthly goals for that big goal? What are your weekly goals? Do you have daily goals? Then, take those steps and put them in your planner. Give yourself ample time to accomplish each step, but also determine when you want to complete your big goal and give yourself a deadline.

As you can see, this blog post is broken into four sections:

- What is Time Blocking?
- Why Should You Use Time Blocking?
- The Pomodoro Method of Time Blocking
- How to Time Block

So right off the bat, I assume I can easily create at least five social media posts and an email newsletter from this blog. I'll do this by simply copying and pasting content directly from the blog and then fleshing it out as needed.

To help showcase exactly how this works, I will give examples below of how I would do this for the above blog post. As I share these examples, I will bold what's been copied and pasted, and anything else is the additions I make for each new piece of content I've created.

Let's start with the email newsletter. All I would do is copy and paste the introduction to the post inside of an email, like so:

I am constantly looking for new ways to manage my time better because I want to get done what needs to be done, but I also want to make sure I have time to tend to myself. Time Blocking has made me more productive and also less frazzled.

Then, I would beef it up just a bit by adding an intro, a little peek into what the rest of the post will be, and a call to action, like so:

Hey, {first_name},

If you're anything like me, you have a million and one things to do but never enough time to do them. And self-care? You know it's important, but who has the time?! Not me, lately. Which is why **I am constantly looking for new ways to manage my time better because I want to get done what needs to be done, but I also want to make sure I have time to tend to myself. Time Blocking has made me more productive and also less frazzled.**

And since it's been so helpful, I want to share it with you. In my latest blog post, I'm covering what it is, why you should use it, and the Pomodoro method, and I even walk you through the how.

You can read the full post here.

And I want to know - have you ever tried time blocking before? How did it work for you? Hit reply and let me know!

It took me less than 3 minutes to write that entire email. Could I have spent more time on it and made it really special? Absolutely. But as you're working to get off the content creation hamster wheel, give yourself the grace to spend as little time repurposing that content as you need. Remember, high-quality, not perfection, here. Just focus on getting consistent and showing up. Over time, you can add some spice.

Now, let's talk about social media captions. Once you've created them, you can use them as is or turn them into a script for video content on a social media platform. Right off the bat, I know I will use the introduction as a new piece of content. I also know that I will use each section of the post as a new post. As I'm creating social media content, I'm doing this similarly to how I did the email newsletters. I copy and paste the bulk of the posts from the blog and add an introduction and a call to action. Sometimes, I'll copy and paste a chunk and then erase parts that aren't necessary for the social media post itself.

Social Media Post #1: Using the Introduction

If you're anything like me, you have a million and one things to do but never enough time to do them. And self-care? You know it's important, but who has the time?! Not me, lately. Which is why I am constantly looking for new ways to manage my time better because I want to get done what needs to be done, but I also want to make sure I have time to tend to

myself. Time Blocking has made me more productive and also less frazzled.

In my latest blog post, I share all about Time Blocking for beginners if you want to hear more about it, but I'm curious to know YOUR favorite productivity tips. Share your top tip in the comments with me.

Social Media Post #2: Section One

My new favorite productivity hack? Time Blocking.○

Time blocking is a type of scheduling that will help you manage your time better. There are two different schools of thought when it comes to Time-Blocking. The first is working by your task, not by the clock.

With this method, you determine your tasks for the day and then work on them until they are complete. Once they're done, you're done working for the day. So if you decide that your tasks are running to the bank, doing a load of laundry, and baking cupcakes for the upcoming bake sale, and you get all that done before noon, then hey, you're done for the day. Typically, if this type of schedule works for you, you wake up motivated to face the day and finish your tasks as soon as possible.

However, I align myself with the second school of thought regarding Time Blocking. For example,this morning, I set aside two hours to work on writing blog posts. Every 25 minutes as I write, I'll get up and walk around and clear my mind for 5 minutes (more on this later in this post), and then I get right back to work. I'll work until those two hours are up, and then it's time to move on to my next block. Whether I finished my tasks or not.

Which do you think you'd prefer? Working by task or by the clock? 🏆

———

Social Media Post #3: Section Two

When I first started Time Blocking, I wasn't scheduling any time to eat or rest in the middle of the day. I learned quickly that this wasn't sustainably, and that it is so easy to put ourselves and our relationships on the back burner behind our to-do lists. We tell ourselves that if we keep going and finish these tasks, we'll have time to relax. But that will never be the case. There will always be something else to do. There will always be a next task. Blocking out my day helps me to purposefully plan time for my priorities and block out the rest of the noise of life.

What's one thing you'd like to make sure you set aside a block of time for each day?

————

Social Media Post #4: Section Three

Have you heard of the Pomodoro Method? It's changed the game for how I stay focused and productive. ⧗

Francesco Cirillo came up with this method in 1992, based on his use of a tomato timer he had. The key feature of this method is the batching of similar tasks within a 25-minute block. After each 25-minute block, there is a 5-minute break. After four twenty-five-minute blocks, you'll take a longer 15-30 minute break.

So when it's time to get to work, set a timer for 25 minutes, and don't allow distractions to pull you out of your groove. After that timer goes off, take a 5-minute break. I prefer to get up and walk around because it rejuvenates me and helps me to be ready to focus for the next 25 minutes. Working at a computer, I often find myself with a slight headache/tension at the end of my block. Then I use those 5 minutes to walk around and do mindless things like picking up this pillow, folding this blanket, etc., which helps clear my mind of the tension.

Plus, it helps my house stay picked up. Otherwise, I have a terrible habit of ignoring the mess until the workday is over and I'm too exhausted to care ... please tell me I'm not the only one. 🫠

———

Social Media Post #5: Section Four

Three steps to start Time Blocking. ⏰

First, look at your non-negotiables. What are the things you can't change or move around? Such as school drop-off and pick-up, work, your gym schedule, church, etc. Put those into your schedule first.

Next, you have to determine your big goals. What are your priorities? What goals surround your priorities? What other plans do you have, or what projects do you want to work on? Set aside time on your schedule to work on those.

And voila! You've got time set aside for yourself (which I hope you put in with your non-negotiables), your commitments, and your goals.

Time Blocking my schedule has been game-changing to help me make progress on my goals. Even if it's not as quick as I'd like - it's nice to see continuous improvement.

If you think you might start Time-Blocking, let me know in the comments.

———

Could you go on to create even more than those five social media posts or that one email? Absolutely. There's no shortage of how you can repurpose your long-form content. But in all likelihood, five is a great goal to set for yourself and more than enough.

Those five posts took me less than five minutes to create, and now I have plenty of content to use to make my long-form content work for me for much longer than I would spend working on it.

Repurposing Audio Content

Now, when it comes to audio content, things aren't quite so simple as cut and paste (unless you transcribe the audio file, which I'll get to in a second), but think along the same general lines of what you'll use from the content and how to use it. You'll likely still want to pull out the introduction and then a tip or small segment from each of the main "sections" of your audio.

When I record my podcast episodes, I work from an outline. Nothing is fully scripted - except for the introduction. I like to write out my introduction because it cuts down on editing, but I also use that introduction for my email and written social media content, just like in the last section.

If you didn't want to work from the outline of what you created, you could transcribe your audio content. Then you can take the exact steps in the "Repurposing Written Content" above to easily repurpose your audio content into written content for your emails and social media. Personally, I get every podcast episode transcribed so that it's more accessible for listeners. At the bottom of every show notes page, you'll find the complete transcription available for reading. A bonus perk to doing that is that it should help your search engine optimization.

That being said, to help get a feel for working from an outline, let's look at what an outline for a podcast episode would look like and how I would use that to repurpose my audio content.

Episode 148: The Part of Your Marketing Plan You Might Be Forgetting

Introduction: How often have you been frustrated because you're putting out content, showing up consistently, and yet not seeing growth in your numbers or business? If you're marketing your business consistently, aren't you supposed to see growth?

And the truth is, yes - and no.

Content marketing is only one-half of a marketing plan. If that's all you're doing to market your business, then you're missing out on part of what should be included in your marketing plan. And no, I'm not talking about paid ads or anything like that. This missing piece is organic marketing as well.

Today I'm going to go over what two parts every marketing plan should have, as well as five of my favorite strategies you can implement for that missing piece.

You're listening to episode 148 of the Chasing Simple Podcast, and I'm your host - Amanda Warfield. This episode was brought to you by the Chasing Simple Content Planner, and you can grab your own atamandawarfield.com/planner/

Outline:

- There are two parts to every marketing plan: nurturing your current audience and growing your audience.

- Nurturing your current audience means showing up for them consistently, giving value and education, and leading them into your sales processes (because remember - marketing and sales aren't the same things)

- Growing your audience means getting out and bringing new people in that you can then nurture

- Sounds simple and self-explanatory, right? But here's the most common misconception I see around this concept: too many entrepreneurs believe that content marketing is a growth strategy.

- Can content grow your audience? Sure. Virality can happen, which will bring in new faces. Your audience might love a piece of your content, and share it, which will lead to growth. But that growth is a byproduct, not a strategy. We all know how impossible it is to predict when a piece of content will be shared on a mass scale. If you can't guarantee you're getting yourself in front of new faces, it's not a growth strategy.

- An exception here would be when you're a first adopter of a new platform. I've talked about this in a few episodes, but we're currently seeing this with Tiktok. Those hopping on early can see viral growth because it's not so crowded yet. So, being an early adopter IS a growth strategy.

- You might be thinking - Okay, Amanda, you've convinced me I must focus on adding growth strategies to my marketing. But what does that look like?

- There are a million and one ways to get yourself in front of a new audience, but let's stick to organic (meaning not paid) marketing.

- Here are my top 5 favorite growth strategies:

1. Pinterest - Listen to Episode 135: Pinterest Best Practices for 2022 with Nadalie Bardo

2. Guesting on other Podcasts or YouTube Shows

3. Guest Teaching in Membership Communities

4. Attending Events and Conferences Where Your Ideal Client/Student Is Attending (Virtual, too)

5. Participating in Bundles

- What's the bottom line on the vast majority of these? Connecting with others in your industry. You cannot do this business thing solo. (Episode 006: Is Isolation Stunting Your Biz Growth?)

- Action Step: Choose ONE growth strategy to implement in the next quarter

---

This episode was meant to encourage listeners to add growth strategies to their marketing plan and introduce them to what that would look like. Like the blog post example, we'll create an email newsletter and five social media posts from this outline. As a reminder, anything in bold was directly copied and pasted from the outline itself. Everything is what I added to flesh out the written content.

For the email, I would directly copy and paste the introduction of the episode to kick things off:

How often have you been frustrated because you're putting out content, showing up consistently, and yet not seeing growth in your numbers or business? If you're marketing your business consistently, aren't you supposed to see growth?

And the truth is, yes - and no.

Content marketing is only one-half of a marketing plan. If that's all you're doing to market your business, then you're missing out on part of what should be included in your marketing plan. And no, I'm not talking about paid ads or anything like that. This missing piece is organic marketing as well.

Today I'm going to go over what two parts every marketing plan should have, as well as five of my favorite strategies you can implement for that missing piece.

Then, I would beef it up just a bit by adding an intro, a little peek into what the rest of the post will be, and a call to action, like so:

Hey there {first_name},

When it comes to your marketing, **how often have you been frustrated because you're putting out content, showing up consistently, and yet not seeing growth in your numbers or business? If**

you're marketing your business consistently, aren't you supposed to see growth?

And the truth is, yes - and no.

Content marketing is only one-half of a marketing plan. If that's all you're doing to market your business, then you're missing out on part of what should be included in your marketing plan. And no, I'm not talking about paid ads or anything like that. This missing piece is organic marketing as well.

What do you need in conjunction with your content? A growth strategy.

In this week's podcast episode, **I'm going over what two parts every marketing plan should have, as well as five of my favorite strategies that you can implement for that missing piece.**

Tune in to discover which of the five will pair best with your content strategy to take your marketing to the next level.

Be sure to come back and let me know which you plan to implement first 😄

Once again, it took me just a couple of minutes to write that entire email out, and it will help to ensure that even more of my audience knows about my latest piece of long-form content. Let's talk about social media and how I'll use the outline to craft five posts.

Social Media Post #1: Using the Introduction

How often have you been frustrated because you're putting out content, you're showing up consistently, and yet you aren't seeing growth in your numbers or business? If you're marketing your business consistently, aren't you supposed to see growth?

And the truth is, yes - and no. 😬

Content marketing is only one-half of a marketing plan. If that's all you're doing to market your business, then you're missing out on part of what should be included in your marketing plan. And no, I'm not talking about paid ads or anything like that. This missing piece is organic marketing as well.

What do you need in conjunction with your content? A growth strategy.

In this week's podcast episode, **I'm going over what two parts every marketing plan should have, as well as five of my favorite strategies that you can implement for that missing piece.**

Head to the link in my bio to discover which of the five will pair best with your content strategy to take your marketing to the next level.

––––––

Social Media Post #2: Topic Introduction

There are two parts to every marketing plan: nurturing your current audience and growing your audience.

Nurturing your current audience means showing up for them consistently, giving value and education, and leading them into your sales processes (typically through your content).

Growing your audience means getting out and bringing new people in that you can then nurture through your content 😁

Sounds simple and self-explanatory, right? But here's the most common misconception I see around this concept: too many entrepreneurs believe that content marketing is a growth strategy.

A growth strategy will require you to get out in front of new audiences, not just the ones you currently have. Some examples would be Pinterest, guest appearances on other business owners' content, guest teaching and speaking, and even attending events where your ideal client will be.

Have you been strategically implementing any growth strategy in conjunction with your content marketing?

———

Social Media Post #3: A List

Not seeing the growth you're hoping to see in your audience? Try adding a growth strategy in conjunction with your content marketing.

Here are my top 5 favorite growth strategies:

1. Pinterest - Listen to Episode 135: Pinterest Best Practices for 2022 with Nadalie Bardo
2. Guesting on other Podcasts or YouTube Shows
3. Guest Teaching in Membership Communities
4. Attending Events and Conferences Where Your Ideal Client/Student Is Attending (Virtual, too)
5. Participating in Bundles

Which one of these sounds most appealing to you?

———

Social Media Post #4: Objection Busting

Can content grow your audience?

Sure. Virality can happen, which will bring in new faces. Your audience might love a piece of your content, and share it, which will lead to growth.

But that growth is a byproduct, not a strategy. We all know how impossible it is to predict when a piece of content will be shared on a mass scale. If you can't guarantee you're getting yourself in front of new faces, it's not a growth strategy.

Consider this your quarterly reminder that your content cannot be the only strategy you have in place for growing your audience.

––––––

Social Media Post #5: Final Thought/Action Step

How often should you be changing up your marketing growth strategy?

My rule of thumb? You don't need a million strategies. You need one that you're focused and intentional with. **Choose ONE growth strategy to implement in the next quarter.**

Then, once you have a firm workflow in place and are confident in your time capabilities for adding in another strategy, add another. But not before. You don't need tons of strategies for growth to see success. You just have to be intentional with the ones you're using.

Want to learn more about my favorite growth strategies? Head over to your favorite podcast player and listen to episode 148 of Chasing Simple.

———

And just like that, in a matter of minutes, you have six pieces of written content that you can use to promote your long-form content over a more extended period of time. In addition to the written content, you can snag audio clips from your audio's introduction and main sections and use those for sound bytes. As social media platforms lean increasingly into video content, this is great because you can upload your sound and overlay it with images, a clip of you working, background scenery, or just about any video that makes sense and captures people's attention.

The best part is that the sound bytes don't need to be long. In fact, they can be really short, which means you can pull out way more than five sound bytes if you want to—making it easy to create many small pieces of content based on one single podcast episode.

Repurposing Video Content

Repurposing your video content will be very similar to repurposing your audio content. Only it will likely be even less work because you won't need to find video or images to go with your sound - you can use the video and audio you already have.

For repurposing video content to written content, you're either working from an outline you created before recording or creating a transcript from the video that you can use to repurpose. Since I've given examples of both of those already, I won't do a complete example again, but here's a quick overview of the steps you would take:

Repurposing From an Outline

STEP ONE: Pull the introduction for the email and one social media post.

STEP TWO: Pull the topic introduction for a social media post.

STEP THREE: Pull a list of teaching points for a social media post.

STEP FOUR: Pull an objection you're busting for a social media post.

STEP FIVE: Pull the final thought/action step for a social media post.

Repurposing from a Transcript

Step One: Transcribe Your Video

Step Two: Pull the introduction for the email and one social media post.

Step Three: Pull the topic introduction for a social media post.

Step Four: Pull a list of teaching points for a social media post.

Step Five: Pull an objection you're busting for a social media post.

Step Six: Pull the final thought/action step for a social media post.

No matter how you're repurposing, you can also think about repurposing sections of your content:

- Introduction
- Main Point One
- Main Point Two
- Main Point Three

- As Many Main Points as You Have
- Closing CTA

Similar to having more options with audio content, a perk of having video content is that you can repurpose it in three different ways. You can use your outline or transcribe the video to create written content. You can pull clips from it to use as is. And you can pull just the audio from it and use it over other images and videos.

Social Media to Social Media Repurposing

Another common way to repurpose your content is by using the same content across multiple social media platforms. In Chapter One, I suggested sticking to one type of social media as you focused on consistency. I'm choosing to believe that you'll heed that advice, and because of that, at some point, you'll make space for yourself or hire help and likely start showing up on more than one social media platform.

When this happens, my advice is always to pick one to go all in on, and for the rest, you'll upload repurposed content you created for your primary platform. So once you've created it once, use it across all platforms.

It should be noted that it won't always be quite as simple as using the exact media for each platform. Attention to detail and understanding of each platform will be necessary for repurposing and reusing content. For example, you may need to resize your graphics or images as different platforms require different sizes. Another example would be that there may be some platforms where you can have a clickable link in a caption, but on others, you need to send someone to your profile to use a link. Small changes like those won't take much time and are worth the effort to get the most out of each platform through repurposing.

When I share this concept with students, I often get asked what happens when an audience member sees the same post from you in multiple places. The truth is, most people aren't following you on every social media channel - they follow you on the one they found you on and stick with that in most cases - unless they're a superfan, in which case, they may follow you in multiple places, but they won't mind seeing repeat content. Or, they may miss it on one platform because of algorithms but will see it on another.

Reusing Content

The final piece of repurposing advice that I have for you is to literally reuse content that you've already created. The vast majority of what you create is only seen/heard/read by a fraction of your audience. And even if they have seen/read/heard it before, they probably don't remember it anyways. Or, they'll pick something new up from it.

A common fear around reusing content is that an audience member will notice that you've said the same thing twice and judge you for it. However, the opposite is true. Most of your audience won't notice, but even if they do, reusing content solidifies you as the expert and what you're saying as something important.

You know how when you rewatch your favorite movie for the 100th time, and you still learn new things about it? Something you never noticed before, or something that hits you differently based on a new phase of life or new life experiences. It's the same thing with your audience and your content. They'll also be catching new things, so if you're going through a period of time where you don't have it in you to create, for whatever reason, this can be your saving grace.

And if that doesn't convince you, maybe this will: these are my insights from a social media post that I completely reused in 2020, five months apart.

Same Post.
5 Months Apart.

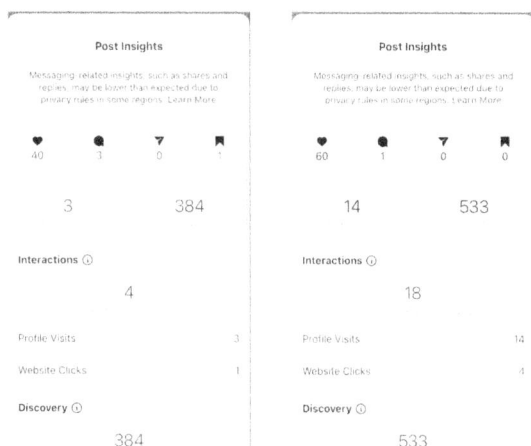

The second time I posted this social media post, the interactions were higher, the reach was higher, and there were significantly more profile visits.

So, how do you do this?

For YouTube videos or podcast episodes, create a quick new intro explaining that this is a re-upload, and you're re-uploading it because of X, Y, Z. Maybe you have a new point you want to add, maybe it's feeling relevant again, and you want to bring it back, maybe it's a favorite piece of content, and you want to make sure new subscribers get to see it.

For blog posts, copy and paste, update it a bit with any additional thoughts you've had on the topic since posting originally, and then re-upload. Bonus points for linking back to the old version, and vice versa, because that's a search engine optimization booster.

And when it comes to social media and email newsletters, copy and paste. Unless it's video content, in which case, download it, find a site that will help remove the watermark if there is one, and re-upload it once more.

Organizing Your Content for Future Re-Sharing

For longevity purposes: don't only repurpose and reuse content right after that piece of long-form content is posted. Is there a month where you're low on time and energy? Go back to the content you've repurposed and share it again. There's no reason why you should only share about a piece of long-form content right as it drops. Share about it three months, six months, a year (or more) later.

Having an organized way to save and store your content will be essential for this practice.

I recommend that you have a master content catalog for easy reference to every piece of content you've created. In my personal spreadsheet, I store the following information:

- Date Published
- SEO Keyword
- Title
- Format (Blog, Podcast, Youtube Video)
- Category (Will Vary by Business. My Categories are Batching, Strategy, Launching, Goals, Time Management, and Sustainability)

- URL
- Offers Linked (Opt-Ins or Paid)

When storing the repurposed content you've created but not posted yet, you could create a Google Doc Folder for Repurposed Content. Within that folder, create a document for each piece of long-form content. Inside that document, list each piece of content that you've repurposed. As you use one, erase it. Once the document is empty, either repurpose more content OR delete it. That way, you've got a folder full of content you can pull from as you plan your content.

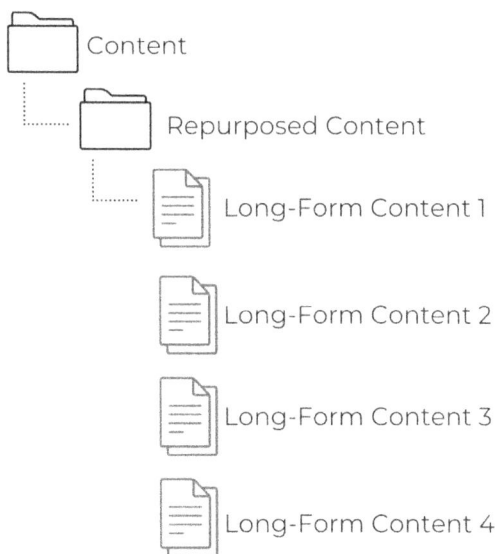

That's why repurposing saves so much time - the bulk of the email? Already written. The topic of the email? Already chosen. The call to action? Already determined. Instead of spending hours writing blog posts/recording podcast episodes/filming YouTube videos for the month, and then hours writing emails, and then hours creating social media content, you spent time creating long-form content. Then you used what you'd already created to create for your other platforms quickly.

Saving you time and mental energy and encouraging your audience to check out the content you've already spent so much time on. Not to mention, it makes it light years easier to show up consistently thanks to being less time-consuming.

Action Step:

Set up a place to store the excess content you will be creating when repurposing.

Additional Resources:

Chasing Simple Episode 155: Keep Your Marketing On Brand (Without Getting Bored)
https://amandawarfield.com/155-2/

For full resources in one place, head to:
https://amandawarfield.com/chasing-simple-marketing-bonuses/

THIRTEEN
BATCH YOUR CONTENT

My husband is a cookie monster. He would easily eat every cookie I make whenever I bake some. It's his absolute favorite treat, and more than once, his birthday cake request has been a Monster Cookie Cake Cheesecake with a cookie cake base and cookies crumbled on top. Every year when we celebrate his getting out of the Navy anniversary? Cookie cake. So, I try to make him cookies every now and then as a surprise. And the last time I made a batch of cookies, it was work, let me tell you.

I pulled out everything I needed - my mixer, paddle attachment, cookie sheet, cooling rack, parchment paper, and all the ingredients I needed to make his favorite cookies.

Then I mixed enough flour, sugar, and other dry ingredients for one cookie. I added in the vanilla and beat in enough egg for one cookie. And then, I scooped the dough for that one cookie into a ball, put it on the baking sheet, and baked it for 10 minutes.

Once it was done, I pulled it out and put it on the cooking rack. Then I started to mix the ingredients for the second cookie. I mixed enough flour, sugar, and other dry ingredients for the second cookie. I added in the vanilla and beat in enough egg for the second cookie. Once it was all mixed evenly, I scooped up that ball of dough, put it on the baking sheet, and baked it for 10 minutes.

Once the ten minutes were up, I put it on the cooling rack with the first cookie and started mixing everything for the third cookie. And on and on that went until I'd made the entire 12 cookies in the batch.

All in all, it took me about 120 minutes just in cooking time to bake the cookies, and then clean up and prep between each one added some time to that. Not bad for a day of baking.

Okay, out of all of the stories I've shared in this book, that was the only one that wasn't real. Except for the "Russell being a cookie monster" part. That's 100% real. But, if I had made that batch of cookies - by piecing the baking out cookie by cookie, I would have spent two hours baking twelve cookies when it could (and should) have only taken ten minutes of baking time.

Baking Individual Cookies

10 minutes from mixing to in the oven   X   12 cookies   =   120 Minutes

Baking a Batch of Cookies

10 minutes from mixing to in the oven   X   1 batch   =   10 Minutes

And the same is true for your content. If you create batches of content, you're going to save yourself significant time and mental energy as well.

The Batching Process

When it comes to batching their content, most people think that means that they're going to sit down and create a bunch of content back to back. That they're going to sit down and outline a blog post, write a blog post, edit that blog post, schedule that blog post, and then do the same with the next one and the next one.

What Batching is Not

Outline Blog Post 1
Draft Blog Post 1
Edit Blog Post 1
Schedule Blog Post 1

Outline Blog Post 2
Draft Blog Post 2
Edit Blog Post 2
Schedule Blog Post 2

Outline Blog Post 3
.....

But in reality, when that's our plan, we most likely get that first blog post scheduled, realize that there are three more to do, and we're already mentally exhausted, so we give up. We tell ourselves that batching doesn't work for us.

The problem? If this is how you're attempting to batch your content - you aren't creating in batches. You're trying to create a ton of content all at once. Like with baking one cookie at a time, you're completing all of the steps before moving on to the next piece. Instead, when batching, we want to create content by step, not by piece.

Using that same blog post example, true batching would look something like this:

STEP ONE: Outline Blog Post One

STEP TWO: Outline Blog Post Two

STEP THREE: Outline Blog Post Three

STEP FOUR: Outline Blog Post Four

STEP FIVE: Write Blog Post One

STEP SIX: Write Blog Post Two

STEP SEVEN: Write Blog Post Three

STEP EIGHT: Wright Blog Post Four

STEP NINE: Edit Blog Post One

And so on and so forth until the four are complete and scheduled. Just like measuring out enough ingredients for a full batch of cookies, you want to start with outlining your full batch of content. Then you'll mix all of the ingredients together (aka writing those first drafts). Next, you'll bake all twelve cookies (or edit all of your content). And finally, you'll cool (or schedule) them all at the same time.

Measure
(Outline)

Mix
(Draft)

Bake
(Edit)

Cool
(Schedule)

Just like baking a dozen cookies can either take you ten minutes or two hours, batching out your content step by step is much more efficient. The reason that batching works so much more efficiently is because of context switching. If you remember the study by Dr. Gloria Mark that I referenced in Chapter Four[4], they found that every interruption of work takes twenty-three minutes and fifteen seconds on average to resume.

This is due to context switching. This is the process of switching your focus from one task to another, and doing so is an interruption to your work. If you switch back and forth multiple times, and each interruption costs you roughly twenty-five minutes, just a few switches easily means saying goodbye to an hour a day or more. However, if you choose one task, you're able to move through it much faster without interruptions, and you save yourself plenty of time (and mental energy).

With that in mind, here's an overview of the batching process:

On the first day of your batch week, you'll need to plan and strategize what content you'll be putting out in the next month.

If you need a tool that will help you lay out your plan and strategize all in one, you may want to grab a copy of the Chasing Simple Content Planner at amandawarfield.com/planner/. I designed it specifically to help you align your content with your business goals so that you were creating a strategy and not just a plan when using it.

The next day of your batch week, you'll create your long-form content. So, you'll either write or record the next month's set of blog posts, podcast episodes, or YouTube videos.

Day three of your batch week means it's time to edit what you did the day before. So you're either editing your blog posts, your podcast episodes, or your YouTube episodes for the month ahead.

Next up comes a day for repurposing. You'll spend day four taking your long-form content apart just like we did together in the last chapter so that you can turn it into your emails and social media content for the next month, with some to store away for future months when you just don't have time to batch your content.

Finally, you have your administrative day. This day is filled with all of the tasks you need to do to wrap up batch week with a bow. You'll create any necessary graphics, upload your long-form content into its appropriate hosting platform, and then schedule every piece of content for the next month. With that, you have an entire month's worth of content created, scheduled, and out of mind so that you can focus on moving the needle in your business.

With this system in place, you're focusing on one single task each day until the final day when you're doing all of your wrap-up administrative tasks. Luckily, those don't take nearly as much brain power as the first four days. By focusing on just one task at a time, you're avoiding the context-switching problem and saving yourself a ton of time, which allows you to only need one week out of each month to create your content for the month ahead.

You may need to customize this batch week schedule to your own business and schedule, which is what I help my students learn to do inside of Content Batching Bootcamp (Learn more at aman dawarfield.com/content/), but this will give you a strong starting point for getting started with this simple, but game-changing, process.

However - while batching may be a simple process, that doesn't make it easy. So let's talk about some of the most common content batching mistakes I see in my students.

Common Batching Mistakes

Batching Too Little Content

Quinn had decided that Monday was going to be the day that she batched out her content. She'd written it in her planner and was fully prepared to create her YouTube video for that Wednesday, her email newsletter for Thursday, and her social media content for Monday, Wednesday, and Friday.

She poured herself a cup of matcha and sat down at her desk as the sun was rising to create her outline for the YouTube video and then map out her newsletter and social media for the week. Once she had it all mapped out, she went to get ready. Then she realized she needed to eat something, so she did that before going back into her office to set up her filming area and equipment. Once that was ready, she reviewed the outline that she had created this morning and got to work filming.

That took a couple of hours, and once it was done, she decided to take a break and have lunch because she was a bit exhausted from all the takes she had to run through. After lunch, she grabbed another matcha and sat down at her desk to start the editing process. After spending a few hours on that, her eyes were burning, and she was mentally exhausted, but hey, the worst was over. So, she got outside to take a walk, and she called her best friend to check-in. Once she was back home, she realized that she needed to get that day's social media post up, so she spent some time writing and creating, and posting it.

She heats leftovers for dinner, changes into her comfy clothes, and settles in front of the TV next to her husband to finish the last of that week's content creation - getting her email newsletter and two other social media posts created and scheduled. She falls into bed that night exhausted but victorious, and really glad she doesn't need to worry about her content again for an entire week because her creativity feels sapped.

There are six problems with this scenario:

1. Not enough time between creation days

I don't know about you, but I'm exhausted from reading that. Quinn spent the entire day creating content, and in this case, the day went perfectly smoothly. She was able to feed herself three meals a day, get some movement in, check in with her best friend, and kind of spend time with her spouse. But we both know that any work day going perfectly smoothly is not the normal. All it would take is one slight distraction to take Quinn from getting in bed victorious to getting in bed overwhelmed and carrying some of her content tasks into the following days. Leading to feeling behind all week. It won't be long before her creativity is completely zapped, and she dreads creating new content because she's spending more days creating content than not.

2. No chance to sit on her content plans

We were all told not to pull all-nighters in college right before a big exam for good reason. Because study after study after study[9] has shown that sleep is linked with better memory retention, and while that may not seem quite relevant to you as a business owner, it does apply in this case. You see, a second issue is that she doesn't allow herself much time to ruminate on what she plans to create. One downside to that is that when you create a plan and an outline and immediately try to record, you're not going to have any of that information really cemented into your brain. Leaving you much more likely to have to run multiple takes to get your information out there.

On top of that, if you don't give yourself enough time and space to mull over what you're planning to create, I can guarantee that, more often than not, you'll think of something in a day or two that you wish you had thought to say or add into your piece of content. While that may not be as big of a deal if you're writing a blog post, when it comes to podcasting or Youtube, you're going to have a lot of extra work to do in order to add that in. Or, in all likelihood, you won't add it in at all.

3. Quality of the content when you're rushing it all into one day

Rushing through creation leads to lower-quality content. When you're rushing through getting your content done as quickly as you can to fit it all into one day, it's not going to be your best work because you're not giving the content, or yourself, time to breathe and rest. Remember, your content is not your entire business, but it is an important part of your business. We want to make sure we're putting out less content that's quality instead of more content that's mediocre.

4. Something will come up.

At some point, Quinn is going to need time off. Whether she plans to take a week off to go on vacation, and she knows ahead of time that she won't be able to create content the following Monday, or whether something unexpected happens, and she has no time to prepare - it's not an "if" but a "when."

Creating content on a weekly basis is not sustainable because something will happen that will prevent you from creating on your normal content day. This leaves you needing to decide, do you set aside another day for content? Or do you skip it for the week? But if whatever takes you out of the office for that content day also takes you out for more than just that day, you're likely going to be playing catch-up once you're back in the office. So, you'll most likely decide to prioritize those takes instead of content - which makes sense - you've got people to serve after all, and that'll set you back another week of content. Once you've finally caught up, you're at two weeks of silence, and you might decide it's been kind of nice not having to create, so you decide to extend your break a little bit longer, which will lead to you all of a sudden popping back up on social media and saying "Hi! Sorry I've been so MIA for the last month .... "

5. Not truly batching.

Frankly, when creating content one week at a time, you're not really batching because you aren't creating a batch of anything. You're just setting aside time to create a bunch of content at once. There's nothing to take step by step because you're creating by piece of content. If you're creating more than one piece of long-form content each week or writing more than one email newsletter, you could argue that I'm wrong. But, if you're creating that much content on a weekly basis, you will, without a doubt, burn out - and probably soon, making the argument null and void anyway.

Plus, just like with the cookies, batching is going to save you time. If you spend eight hours every Monday for an entire month working on content, that's 32 - 40 hours a month. If you set aside a week each month, you're going to be able to finish your content batching in just a few hours each day, thanks to repetitive steps taking less time than creating whole pieces at once. I spend about four hours a day each day during batch week creating content. That's only twenty hours a month instead of those 32 - 40 hours.

Not to mention, there are some tasks that when you "batch" on a weekly basis, you'll have to do four to five times a month, but when you batch on a monthly basis, you'll only have to do once. Like setting up your filming equipment (or laying out blankets all over the subfloor in your office because a dog peed on all of your carpets). It may not seem like it takes a lot of time, but that time does add up. Although, I think we can all agree that not having to get fully camera ready every single Monday would save a mega-ton of time.

6. Extra content weeks.

And then, there are the weeks when you're going to need to create extra content. Whether for a launch or for a project or event that you're working on - sometimes we need to put out extra content. If you're already maxing yourself out each Monday, where are you going to find the time to create that extra content? When it comes to launches, there's a lot of extra content to create, and if you don't give yourself time to create it and schedule it out during your batch week, you're going to run into massive issues during the launch. Instead of protecting your time and your mental health, you're going to have to be working on creating that content throughout the launch period, leaving you all the more likely to not follow through with the launch and see it to completion. But that's a topic for a different book.

The bottom line is that by only creating one week's worth of content at a time, Quinn is setting herself up for failure. But if, instead, she set aside one week each month to create an entire month's worth of content, she'd be able to show up consistently for her audience in less time and with less mental fatigue.

Not Setting Aside the Time for It

Brooke is a busy mom of two and runs her business in the cracks of the day - before the kids wake up, during nap time, and after they're in bed. She's been batching her content on a monthly basis for a few months now and has already seen what it can do for her business. Even though she only has a few hours a day to work, in the last few months, she's been able to complete projects that have been on her project management board for over a year, her revenue is up, and all the while, she's spending less time and energy on creating content than ever before.

Her next batch is supposed to be happening this week, but day one got off to a slow start because the boys had a doctor's appointment that threw off their nap schedule. On day two, she finally got started and made good progress on what she was supposed to do on day one. She figured that being one day behind wasn't the end of the world and that she'd still be able to tackle her plan with no problem. Only then she remembered that on day four, she's also got a hair appointment that will disrupt her work time. And on day five, she's skipping her normal work time in the evening to have dinner with her friends while her spouse stays home with the boys.

All of a sudden, batch week was over, and the progress she made was minimal. Not only did nothing get scheduled, but Brooke is feeling frustrated and overwhelmed because now she's got to somehow figure out when to create the content that didn't get created this week, but also, next week's to-do list is up in the air. Can she actually get done what she wants to get done?

The problem? Brooke didn't set aside intentional time for her batch week. This is a common scenario my students find themselves in. They start batching, love it, and start seeing results. But once the newness wears off, it quickly becomes just another item on the to-do list. They have a general plan for when they'll have their batch week, but they don't protect that time. So when batch week starts, they realize they have appointments, meetings, and deadlines all that week that can't be rearranged.

Instead, whatever type of calendar you use - paper or digital - mark off your batch week on it now. For all of the months of the rest of the year and potentially even into next year. Put your batch week on the calendar, but also do what you can to close that week off. If you're a paper planner person, take washi tape and run it across that entire week. If you're a digital calendar person, close that week, so no one can set appointments or meetings. It may not seem like much, but putting up those boundaries will make a big difference in your time management for a batch week. When you go to try and schedule something, you'll see the boundaries you put up, and it's going to make you reconsider.

Now, sometimes, there's no other option. If you've been trying to get into a doctor for months and their only availability is during batch week, or your child gets sick and has to come home from school - there's not much you can do about that. But if you're protecting your time and aren't putting just anything on the calendar during batch week, it will really help. Not to mention, having one or two other things on the schedule likely isn't going to make a huge difference. The problem comes when you fill the schedule for the week and try to fit batch week into the cracks of the week. It's not going to work out that way.

Not Simplifying

Haley is as type A as they come - an Enneagram One, a perfectionist - she's always trying to do too much, yet feeling like she's never doing enough. That shines through all too clearly when it comes to her content. She's building her side hustle and, at the same time, working a full-time job teaching. She's committed to a batch week, but month after month, she isn't quite able to get it all done. She's trying to put out a new podcast episode every week, plus a blog post for each podcast episode, an email newsletter every Wednesday, and a social media post six days a week. Somehow, even with her batch week, she can't seem to get it all done and scheduled, leading to her needing to set aside two weeks each month for batching her content. And that means she's behind on client work, so she fills as much of her time with that as she can outside of batch week, and all of a sudden? It's batch week all over again, she hasn't had a chance to rest her creativity muscles, and once again, she didn't have any time to work on any of her needle-moving projects in her business.

Haley's problem is that she hasn't simplified enough. She's trying to do too much. She's a solopreneur with limited time, and yet she's spending half of her working hours simply on creating content. And while, yes, content marketing is an important part of her business (especially without a marketing budget), it's not her entire business. Unfortunately, working like this means she's not leaving herself much time to get other work done - especially when you consider the need for leaving space to take time off. To have white space. To rest. To relax. To go on vacation. To get sick. To have sick kids. It's not often that we, as entrepreneurs, ever actually work four full forty-hour work weeks during a month. And that's okay. The flexibility of entrepreneurship is likely what drew most of us to this path. It's important to take time off. That's not the problem. The problem is that Haley has left herself with not enough time to do so and also move the needle in her business.

In theory, you should be moving the needle in your business more than you are marketing. And by you, I mean you as the CEO, not the business in general. But for now, as a solopreneur, they're one and the same. At some point, you might love to hire a full-time marketing team, but we aren't there yet. And if you take into account the need for time off, you can roughly outline a month like this: one week for time off, one week for content, and two weeks for needle-moving tasks. Really, no matter how you configure it - if you're setting aside two weeks each month for content batching, you're going to be spending the same amount of time, if not more, creating content than you are moving the needle in your business.

So, instead, set aside one week per month for your content batching. If you're continuously not able to complete your batch week - you're trying to create too much content. Simplify even further and ask yourself where you can show up even less. Instead of creating four pieces of long-form content a month, cut it down to two in order to make it possible to create a month's work in that one week. And if you really want to fast-track your growth, instead of pouring two weeks each month into your content marketing, pour one week into content and another into some of those other ways to see growth in conjunction with your content that I went over in Chapter Five.

Waiting Until Inspired

Peyton is a creative to her core. She didn't start her business because she wanted to start her business. She started her business because she loved her art, and then that evolved into a business. She knows how important marketing is, but it's hard not to treat it just like her creative process for her work. She prefers to only post something when she's feeling inspired and has a hard time creating otherwise, which has led her to show up inconsistently and with long stretches of silence when the inspiration just isn't there.

The thing about content marketing is that it's both an art and a science. You can't view it through the lens of just one or the other. In Peyton's case, she's viewing it strictly as an art and only ever creating when she's inspired and about what she's inspired by. Not only does this lead to gaps and inconsistencies, but it also leads to an audience that's confused and unsure of what she's an expert on. Remember, in Chapter Twelve, we talked about the importance of consistency in messaging and how that showcases us as the expert? Well, if you're only ever posting what you're inspired to post, there's most likely not going to be any cohesive trail of content for your audience to follow.

On the other hand, some people look at content marketing strictly through the lens of science. They only focus on the data, the numbers, and repurposing content that has already been created. And while all those things are important for understanding what your audience is interacting with and keeping things simple, it is important to be inspired by what you're creating. Or create after becoming inspired. Because when you're inspired, you're more likely to truly connect with someone new in your audience. The content you're passionate about creates connection, and the content you're creating just because it's fun or you want to bring out your personality in your content leads to further connection. The bottom line is that while the strategy is important, so is having fun with your marketing.

But how do we blend the two together? As with most things in life, it's a balancing act. This means that it's not a black-and-white system to follow step by step. However, I do have some tips to help you cultivate content that's both inspirational and strategic while still utilizing batch weeks.

First, when you're feeling really inspired to create something, go ahead and do it. (Unless you're simply procrastinating ... we both know what I mean here). There's no rule that says you can only create during batch week. In fact, when you begin to implement a batch week, you'll likely find that you're more inspired than ever now that you don't have to constantly force yourself to create. Once you've created whatever you were inspired to create, you can do one of two things with it. If it's timely, go ahead and post it. There's no rule that says you only need to post what you created during batch week. The goal of batch week is to make sure you're showing up consistently and not ghosting your people. It's okay to put bonus content out there into the world.

The other option is to save it and use it for next month's content. If it's not timely, this is usually my go-to. That way, during my next batch week, that's one less piece of content that I need to create. Just like I save content I've repurposed, I also save content I create when inspired for future use. Anytime I'm inspired or think of a topic I want to cover, I open up my Trello board and pop it inside. And yes, there are entire captions inside of that board that I can simply copy and paste into my plan whenever I need a little something extra. This is especially helpful when a month comes around that's extra busy or when I'm feeling absolutely zero creativity. I can use or re-use what's on that board in order to get the content out there with the least amount of mental energy.

Setting aside one week every month to intentionally batch out the month's content is the number one thing you can do to show up consistently. It allows you three weeks of not having to think about content marketing for your business. Yet, you're still showing up consistently for your audience and building the Know, Like, and Trust factor. You're pulling in new leads by sending them to your long-form content, which will likely send them to a way to get on your email list or purchase from you. For those three weeks, your business is marketing itself, and you're able to move the needle on other projects behind the scenes, serve your people well, and, even more importantly - rest and be present for yourself and your loved ones.

Action Step:

Put your next batch week, and all of your batch weeks for the remainder of the year, on your calendar.

Additional Resources:

Chasing Simple Episode 024: How to Create a Month's Worth of Content in One Week
https://amandawarfield.com/024-2/

Chasing Simple Content Planner
https://amandawarfield.com/planner/

Content Batching Bootcamp
https://amandawarfield.com/content/

For full resources in one place, head to:
https://amandawarfield.com/chasing-simple-marketing-bonuses/

CONCLUSION - WHAT'S NEXT?

Before I even came up with the outline for this book, all I had was an idea. A vague inkling of what it was that I wanted to write about. And along with that idea, I had a lot of fear. Could I actually write something worth reading? Who am I to write a book? Why would anyone pick up my book off the shelf and read what I have to say? Would I even be able to finish a rough draft? But outside of that fear, I also had so much love for the person I wanted to write this book for... And that love is what got me started and kept me going as I got into the writing process, and the fears continually piled on top of each other.

Before I even began to brainstorm what was going to go into this book, I sat down to journal through my thoughts and prayed over the words I was going to write and the person I was writing this book for - aka you. Here's an excerpt from those journal pages:

I want to help the solopreneur that I was. The one that started a tiny side hustle with huge dreams and no idea how to get there or what the steps were. The one that had no back-ground in business, that didn't have an MBA but did have something to share with the world. The one that was so confused about marketing and completely overwhelmed by all of the must-dos and things to keep track of that she spent all of her time working on marketing (not seeing growth) and none on actually building and growing a business. The one that spent all of her time trying to grow an audience, thinking that was how you get clients. I want to simplify the starting steps for solopreneurs in the online space to ease some of their anxiety and imposter syndrome. Their fears and worries. And maybe even shorten the time it takes to reach "success." There are so many books out there for the already successful. I want to write something for everyone. Something even (and especially) a new solopreneur can put into practice so that their marketing can be simple from the start.

I also journaled about what the purpose behind the book was:

Help make content marketing and creation simple. So that solopreneurs can fit marketing into their business without it taking over their business. So that they can run the business they're dreaming of and pursue their dream life.

Then, at the beginning of the book, I made this promise: "I promise that as you read this book and hear my stories, you're going to get the vulnerable truth. I promise that you're going to walk away feeling confident about your content marketing. And I promise you'll walk away with an actionable plan to simplify your marketing so that you can fit it into your business without it taking over your business."

Then we started with a crash course in content marketing. This foundational section helped you decide where you're going to be showing up with content, where to focus your time and attention and where not to, how to show up for your current audience while also growing your audience and the difference between creating a content plan and creating a content strategy.

After that, we discussed the three phases of a business journey. We went over what those phases look like, what the overarching business goal is, and how to be intentional about that goal in relation to your marketing strategy, including your nurture strategy for your content and your growth strategies for other marketing opportunities.

Finally, we honed in on consistency. Because while it's a simple way to see growth in your business, it's not always a simple practice. Which is why I covered three tactics, in detail, that will help you simplify your marketing efforts, so you can show up consistently - helping you find a balance between marketing and other business efforts. Where your marketing is truly getting you your biggest bang for your buck (that buck being your time). Where you're spending enough time marketing to see growth but not so much you're seeing diminishing returns on what you're putting out. And where you're able to feel confident showing up while also moving the needle as a solopreneur. Instead, you're able to take the time and mental energy you've been spending on marketing and putting it towards needle-moving strategies and projects in your business, which will also help you see an increase in your bottom line.

As you've gone through each chapter, I hope you've taken the time to complete the action steps I gave you because those action steps are the actionable plan I promised to give you to simplify your marketing. But, in case you didn't, let's quickly recap that plan now.

STEP ONE: Take a minute and journal what you hope to accomplish once you've learned how to best leverage your marketing.

STEP TWO: Choose the platforms you'll be showing up on moving forward. Remember, these aren't permanent and can change in the future, but decide what's reasonable for you for the time being.

STEP THREE: Give yourself permission to start without understanding everything. Truly, take a piece of paper and write, "I can serve others right where I am," and then post it somewhere where you'll see it. You don't have to have it all figured out in order to serve your people well.

STEP FOUR: Take some time and free-flow journal out your thoughts around your business mission (who you want to help and how) and your personal values. If you have any thoughts as to what your business core values might be, journal those too. If you don't, no big deal - remember that it's okay to let those evolve over time.

STEP FIVE: Stop spending time on practices that attempt to "hack" your way to growth, worrying about the algorithm, cold messaging, and bots, and focusing on trends.

STEP SIX: Choose one growth strategy to begin applying alongside your content marketing.

STEP SEVEN: Take the "Marketing Strategies to Use Based on Your Phase of Business" Quiz.

STEP EIGHT: Find a networking group in your area. I strongly recommend trying to find a Rising Tide Society chapter near you.

STEP NINE: Download and fill out the worksheet I created for you to dig deeper into the problem you solve and how it helps your audience.

STEP TEN: Download and fill out the Customer Journey Cheat Sheet.

STEP ELEVEN: It's time to create another important reminder for yourself. Take out a piece of paper and write: "Consistency ≠ Constant." Then, stick it on your monitor or your laptop so you're sure to see it often.

STEP TWELVE: Cut down on the number of platforms you're showing up on and how often you're showing up on them.

STEP THIRTEEN: Set up a place to store the excess content you will create when repurposing.

STEP FOURTEEN: Put your next batch week, and all of your batch weeks for the remainder of the year, on your calendar.

Once you complete all fourteen action steps, you'll be well on your way to fitting your marketing into your business without it taking over your business.

Take the Next Step

If you're reading this book, you're likely a solopreneur on a tight budget, which is why your marketing is falling on you and why it's so important to make sure that you're not spending all of your time and energy on marketing. You've got a lot to do and never enough time to do it all. In order to see business growth, you've got to market yourself, but you've also got to *continue* to market yourself once you start seeing that growth. The content creation hamster wheel can truly be never ending once you find yourself stuck on it.

These action steps are going to help you get off, but I'd love to see you *stay off*.

As your business continues to grow and evolve, you might choose to start handing off bits and pieces of your marketing. Personally, my batch weeks have shifted tremendously over the years. I spent the first three years of business doing it all on my own. I started small, and over time, as I became more efficient, I was able to add more and more content to my plan each month.

Then, I outsourced my podcast editing. I'd reached a point where I was bringing in a semi-consistent income, and I quickly was becoming annoyed with that aspect of creating my content. So, I decided to give outsourcing a trial run. It was such a relief to be able to not have to edit any longer. And for two years, that was the only help I brought on because the budget wasn't there for any additional help.

Next, I hired a Virtual Assistant specifically to come in and schedule the content for me. I'm still doing the planning, the strategy, and the creation, but my VA helps minimize my time spent on content by scheduling it all out for me. That way, I have even more time to work on needle-moving projects. As of writing this, my VA is only helping out five hours a month. Over time, I'd love to bump that up significantly, but like with your content, starting small is key. Once I'm able to handle more hours in my budget, and once I'm able to work on offloading new tasks, we'll add in more hours. And I'm sure this will not be the final part of my marketing that I outsource - even as a marketing and launch strategist.

Some people also choose to hire Social Media Managers that take the entire burden of their social media off of them. Or, they decide to hire platform-specific experts to completely offload a platform they aren't interested in but want to show up on.

And some, like my own clients, decide to outsource the strategy and beyond. I have clients that hire me to come up with the strategy and plan, and then they take that plan and create content themselves. Others hire me to create the plan *and* the content. And even others that take the plan we create and pass it off to their own Virtual Assistant. There are many different ways you can get help with creating content.

Over time, you're going to be able to spread your wings with your marketing and hire help in order to see even more growth. But, for now, you're going to want to start small and focus on showing up consistently in those few areas you decided on back in Chapter One. At this point, the number one obstacle that arises is that business owners will get excited, they'll start showing up consistently, and then life happens, and they fall off the train and end up right back on the hamster wheel. If you're reading this and wondering how you can avoid that fate, this is exactly why I created my course - Content Batching Bootcamp.

Content Batching Bootcamp is an online course that helps entrepreneurs create a content batching system that's unique to their own business and get off the content creation wheel by becoming consistent with their content - in order to build relationships with their audience and grow their bottom line. So that they can build the business that will support their dream life.

Students inside of Content Batching Bootcamp learn how to create a batching system that works for their unique business (whether they work five hours a week or forty), and they have seen remarkable results from only having to create content once a month.

Like Laura of Laura Murray Creative, whose batching week only took her half a day each day and enabled her to create a manageable plan for her content and her time. One that she can execute with much less stress.

Or Sarah of Sarah Ever After, who saw a 35% increase in traffic to her site, an increase in affiliate income, and a 10% increase in followers on Instagram in just her first month of batching. Oh, and Sarah works VERY part-time in her business, as she homeschools her son the majority of her time.

My goal is to help you build relationships with your audience to grow your business. If creating strategic content without taking forever is a priority, and you're serious about investing time, money, and energy into your business in order to make it a success, the best first step is to learn more about Content Batching Bootcamp.

If you're ready to get started and think you might like to work with me and join hundreds of other entrepreneurs working towards the same goals as you, go ahead and check out Content Batching Bootcamp at amandawarfield.com/content/

I'm on a mission to help solopreneurs live their dream life by simplifying their content marketing to fit their marketing into their business without it taking over their business, and I hope you'll be one of those.

And if you'd like help showing up consistently, I'd love to see you inside my course, Content Batching Bootcamp.

Get to Work

As Walt Disney once said, "If you can dream it, you can do it." I've held this quote in the back of my mind since day one of building my business. In fact, the first journal I was using when I started my business had that quote on the cover. And as I was dreaming of what this business might be inside of those pages and despairing over what it sometimes felt like it would never be ... that quote kept me going.

And now, here I am, six years later, running a business that was more than I ever dreamed of. A business that replaced my teaching salary. A business that allows me to flexibly shift my schedule with my husband's. A business that enables me to travel to my heart's (well, okay, my wallet's) desire. A business that has brought so many incredible opportunities and people into my life. I've spoken on stage. I've visited new places. I've written an entire book, with plans for at least one more. The opportunities have been more than I ever could have expected.

No matter where you are today in your business, I promise that all this is possible for you, too. I'm not special. I don't have a business degree. I'm just a quirky, introverted girl with a big dream who keeps taking the next step. And it all started with showing up consistently with my marketing.

Start showing up for your audience consistently and taking steps forward each day, and you'll be able to do whatever it is that you're dreaming of too.

LOVE AND CAT-HAIR HUGS,

AMANDA

Action Step:

Learn more about Content Batching Bootcamp by heading to *amandawarfield.com/content/* and use code READER to save on your enrollment.

Additional Resources:

The Chasing Simple Podcast
https://amandawarfield.com/chasing-simple/

For full resources in one place, head to:
https://amandawarfield.com/chasing-simple-marketing-bonuses/

PS If you enjoyed this book and saw success from taking these steps, it would mean the world to me if you would leave a review on Amazon and/or GoodReads. Reviews help get the book into the hands of more readers and help those on the fence about giving it a try decide if it's right for them.

ACKNOWLEDGEMENTS

When I began the undertaking of writing this book, I knew I would need help. But I severely underestimated just how far that help and support would go. I'm quite certain this book would not exist without the assistance of so many.

To Jodi Brandon, of Jodi Brandon Editorial, without your incredible insights, this book wouldn't be half the book it is today. Your gentle leading and thoughtful edits and suggestions helped guide me to completely rip apart everything I'd done and create this much more powerful book.

To Dana Ellington, of Nowata Press Publishing & Consulting, thank you for taking the time to go through and highlight my grammar mistakes. Without you, this book would not feel nearly half as professional as it does now.

To Laura Murray, of Laura Murray Creative, thank you for taking my ideas and making this book feel real for the very first time with your beautiful cover designs. I still mourn many of them - if only a book could have multiple covers!

To Haylee Gaffin and Megan Wren, of Gaffin Creative, your exper-tise made the audiobook possible, and I'm forever grateful to both of you for that. Not only that, but without the two of you, the podcast would not still exist. You're a huge cog in making my business run smoothly, and I'm eternally grateful for everything you do.

To Jennifer Gregson, my right-hand lady, there are no words to thank you for all that you do for me. Your insight into the publishing world was instrumental in making this book happen, but having you in my corner day in and day out, even more so. I can honestly say this book would not exist without you.

To my Launch Team, your willingness to share about Chasing Simple Marketing has been humbling. I am eternally grateful to each of you for helping me get the word out there about this book.

To my Beta Readers - Alyson, Amy, Emily, Erin, Jessica, Kayla, Laken, Lydia, Mara, Melissa, Sabrina, and Sharon - your willingness to read the roughest of rough drafts and leave comments and critiques was more helpful than I could express. You let me know which jokes fell flat, and which ones came through, what felt relat-able and what didn't. The final version is massively different than what you originally read, and infinitely better, thanks to you.

To everyone who voted on some aspect of the book - Thank you for your willingness to be involved. Every vote, every DM, I truly trea-sured and those helped this book become what it is today.

To all the readers, especially those of you who are actually reading this page, the gratitude I have for you is immeasurable. You are who I wrote this book for, and I have so much love in my heart for you. I cannot wait to see how your business grows and flourishes over the years.

To all of my friends that have repeatedly asked questions about the book, I'm sorry I have such a hard time talking about the big, scary things I'm working on. Your support truly does mean the world to me - even when I don't know how to express it and change the subject instead.

To my Girardeau Family, thank you for not batting an eye when I suddenly announced in our group text that I was creating "Girardeau Publishing", and then asked you to vote on entirely too many different logo options. To my dad, for instilling the entrepreneurial spirit in me and showing me what it looks like to chase big dreams. To Gaga and Grandaddy for ... well, more than I could even begin to put into words. From playing countless hours of "waitress" with me, to ensuring I didn't take on any student loan debt ... I cannot imagine being blessed with two more loving grandparents. Sunday afternoons with you are one of the best parts of my week. To my aunts and uncles for helping to raise me into the person I am today. To my cousins, for always feeling more like siblings. And to my siblings, we'll always have each other. I love each of you more than words can express.

To my Warfield Family, thank you for accepting me into your family with so much love. Growing up, I always loved being part of a big family, and all I ever wanted from my husband's family was to fit in and feel welcomed. Since before we even met, you've made me feel like I was loved as one of you and I am eternally grateful for that. It's been nothing short of pure joy to have gained another set of aunts, uncles, and cousins. To Greg and Christina, thank you for raising such an incredible man, and for loving me as your own. And to Nick, Kier, Sam, and Marissa, I love y'all as if you were my own blood siblings. Here's to many more adventures together.

And to Russell. I could write pages on all of the ways you helped make this book possible. Thank you for making sure I feed myself when I'm entirely too wrapped up in work, for making me laugh when I overthink and overstress, and thank you for always supporting the wild ideas I throw out into the world. Who knew that when you supported me starting a blog all those years ago, that we would one day end up here?

Appendix

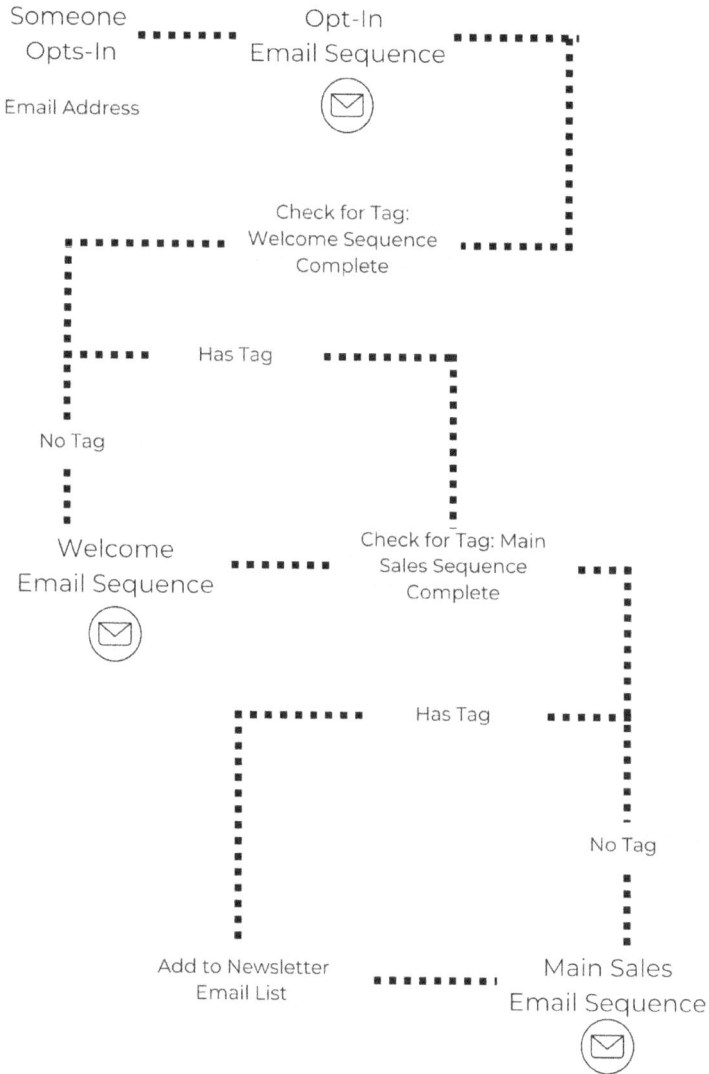

Someone Opts-In

Email Address

Opt-In Email Sequence

Check for Tag:
Welcome Sequence
Complete

Has Tag

No Tag

Welcome Email Sequence

Check for Tag: Main
Sales Sequence
Complete

Has Tag

No Tag

Add to Newsletter
Email List

Main Sales
Email Sequence

NOTES

[1] "marketing noun - Definition, pictures, pronunciation and usage notes | Oxford Advanced American Dictionary at OxfordLearners-Dictionaries.com." n.d. Oxford Learner's Dictionaries. Accessed April 15, 2023. https://www.oxfordlearnersdictionaries.com/us/definition/american_english/marketing.

[2] "Ecommerce Market Data and Ecommerce Benchmarks for February 2023." n.d. IRP Commerce. Accessed April 15, 2023. https://www.irpcommerce.com/en/gb/ecommercemarketdata.aspx.

[3] "Home." n.d. Google. Accessed April 15, 2023. https://www.google.com/search?rlz=1C1JZAP_enUS974US974&q=community&si=AMnBZoH8-oCWwoiwSeTBG9z_l7xBJH5uZvxPU3ZFmxTN4eLCyqIeTAK4LEaU-CcK7SDBQ85czHhc_MprrStVMDFnwiUbg-_NoQB8f8RQccmWiBYOAbV3onA%3D&expnd=1&sa=X&ved=2ahUKEwi6-7Kw3Kv-AhVjtoQIHVkgAfcQ2v4IegUIGRC-A.

[4] Robinson, Jennifer. 2006. "Too Many Interruptions at Work?" Gallup News. https://news.gallup.com/businessjournal/23146/too-many-interruptions-work.aspx.

[5] Whitler, Kimberly. n.d. "Home." Why Word Of Mouth Marketing Is The Most Important Social Media. Accessed April 15, 2023. https://www.forbes.com/sites/kimberlywhitler/2014/07/17/why-word-of-mouth-marketing-is-the-most-important-social-media/?sh=410845b154a8.

[6] Gray, Colin. n.d. "Podcast Statistics & Industry Trends 2023: Listens, Gear, & More." The Podcast Host. Accessed April 15, 2023. https://www.thepodcasthost.com/listening/podcast-industry-stats/.

[7] "Podcast Statistics & Figures 2020 - Discover the Best Podcasts." n.d. Discover Pods. Accessed August 3, 2022. https://discoverpods.com/podcast-statistics/.

[8] "Marketing Rule of 7's." n.d. Illumination Marketing. Accessed April 15, 2023. https://www.marketingillumination.com/single-post/marketing-rule-of-7s.

[9] Potkin, K. T., & Bunney, W. E., Jr (2012). Sleep improves memory: the effect of sleep on long term memory in early adolescence. *PloS one*, 7(8), e42191. https://doi.org/10.1371/journal.pone.0042191

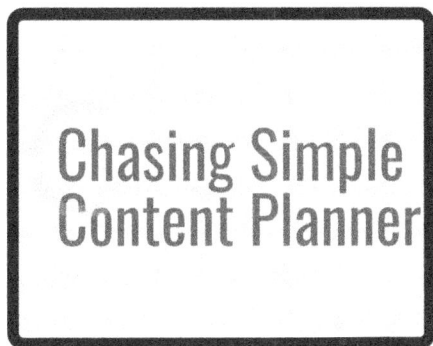

Looking for a simple way to organize your content marketing strategy?

Get a copy of the Chasing Simple Content Planner:

AMANDAWARFIELD.COM/CONTENT

Please Leave a Review

Thank you so much for reading Chasing Simple Marketing!

I love hearing what readers have to say about the book, and your feedback will help to make future versions of this book, and other future books, even better.

For authors, reviews matter a *lot*, and each one makes a difference - including yours.

If you could take two minutes right now to leave a review on Amazon, or on GoodReads (*or both!*) to let me know what you thought about the book, it would mean the world to me.

I'm so grateful to you for being here. Thank you for being part of this journey.

AMANDA

AUTHOR BIO

Amanda Warfield traded in her classroom lesson plans for an online blog that she had no idea how to turn into a business. Six years later, she's a speaker, author, educator, host of the Chasing Simple podcast, and spends her time helping other entrepreneurs sustainably fit their marketing into their business, without it taking over their business - so that they can grow their business.

As a simplicity-focused content marketing and launch strategist, she helps entrepreneurs craft their content strategy, write their copy, and simplify their launches.

Amanda currently lives in Aiken, SC with her husband and their two cats, and if she could, she would spend all of her time watching Gamecock sports and reading in their hammock.